Help Me! Guide to the iPad Air

By Charles Hughes

Table of Contents

Getting Started

Table of Contents

1. Button Layout

The iPad has three buttons, one switch, and two jacks. The rest of the functionality is controlled by the touchscreen. Each button has several functions, depending on the context in which it is used. The iPad buttons perform the following functions:

Figure 1: Front View

Home Button - Returns the iPad to the Home screen at any time.

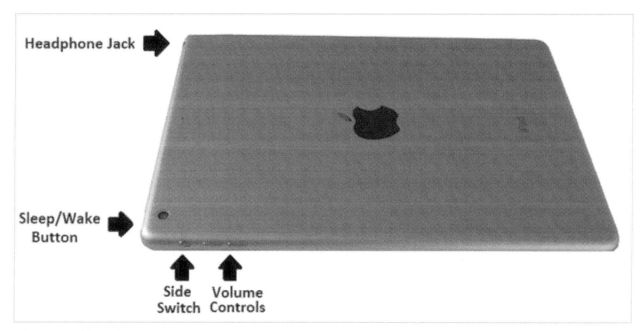

Figure 2: Rear View

- **Headphone Jack** - Allows headphones to be connected.
- **Sleep/Wake Button** - Turns the iPad on and off, or locks and unlocks the device.
- **Volume Controls** - Increases and decreases the media volume.
- **Side Switch** - Turns the Mute function on and off, or locks and unlocks screen rotation, depending on the settings. Refer to *"Changing the Function of the Side Switch"* on page 229 to learn how to adjust the Side Switch settings.

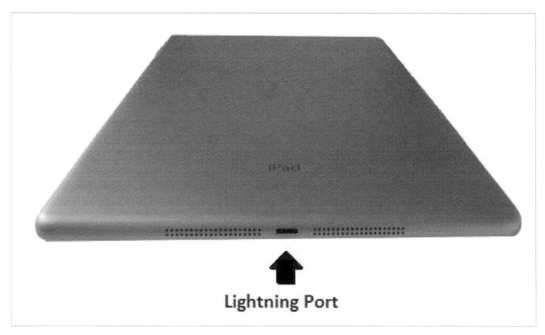

Lightning Port

Figure 3: Bottom View

- **Lightning Port** - Connects the iPad to a computer in order to transfer data. It also connects the iPad to a charger.

2. Turning the iPad On and Off

Use the Sleep/Wake button to turn the iPad on or off. To turn the iPad on, press and hold

the **Sleep/Wake** button for two seconds. The iPad turns on and the logo is displayed. After the iPad has finished starting up, the Lock screen is displayed.

Note: If the iPad does not turn on after a few seconds, try charging the battery.

To turn the iPad off, press and hold the **Sleep/Wake** button until "Slide to power off" appears at the top of the screen. Touch and hold **Slide to power off** and move your finger to the right. The iPad turns off.

Note: To keep the iPad on, press "Cancel" or do not take any action at all.

3. Navigating the Screens

There are many ways to navigate the iPad. Use the following tips to quickly navigate the screens of the iPad:

- Use the **Home** button to return to the Home screen at any time. Any application or tool that you were using will be in the same state when you return to it.
- At the Home screen, slide your finger to the left to access additional pages. If nothing happens, the other pages are blank.
- Touch the center of any Home screen and slide your finger down to access the iPad's search feature. You may search any data stored on your iPad, including application data. Touch the center of the Home screen again and slide your finger up to hide the search field.

4. Setting Up Wi-Fi

Use a nearby Wi-Fi hotspot or a home router to avoid having to use data. Wi-Fi is required to download some large applications. To turn on Wi-Fi:

1. Touch the ⚙ icon. The Settings screen appears, as shown in **Figure 4**.
2. Touch **Wi-Fi**. The Wi-Fi Networks screen appears, as shown in **Figure 5**.
3. Touch the ⬭ switch next to 'Wi-Fi'. Wi-Fi turns on and a list of available networks appears, as shown in **Figure 6**. If the network has an 🔒 icon next to it, a password is needed to connect to it.
4. Touch the network to which you would like to connect. The Wi-Fi Password prompt appears if the network is protected, as shown in **Figure 7**.
5. Enter the network password. Touch **Join** in the bottom right-hand corner of the screen. Provided that you entered the correct password, a check mark appears next to the network name and the 📶 icon appears at the top of the screen. You are connected to the Wi-Fi network.

Note: If you enter an incorrect password, the message "Unable to join the network >Network Name<" appears, where '>Network Name<' is the name of your network. The network password is usually written on the modem given to you by your internet service provider. It is sometimes called a WEP Key.

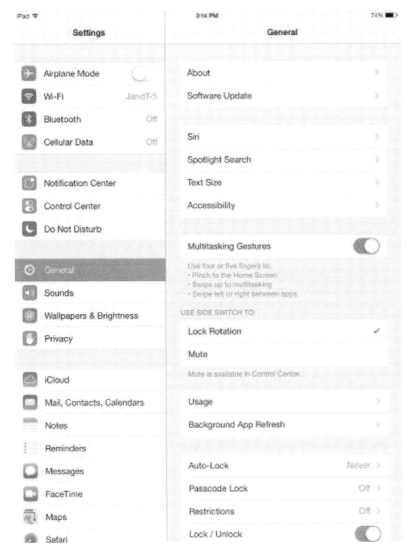

Figure 4: Settings Screen

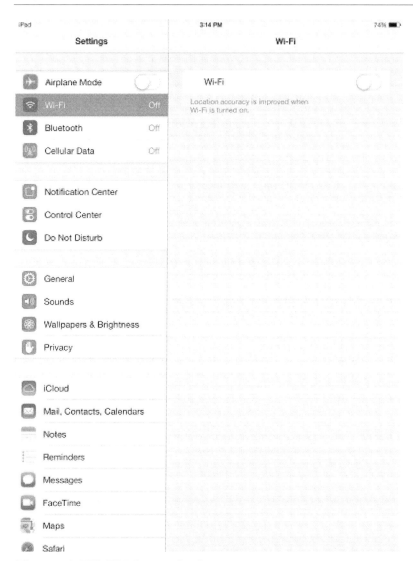

Figure 5: Wi-Fi Networks Screen

Figure 6: List of Available Wi-Fi Networks

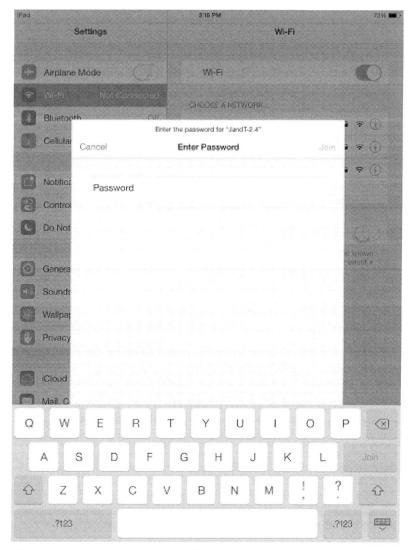

Figure 7: Wi-Fi Password Prompt

5. Setting Up an Email Account

You must set up your email account before you can use the Mail application on your iPad. Make sure that Wi-Fi is turned on before attempting to set up an email account. Refer to *"Setting Up Wi-Fi"* on page 12 to learn how to turn on Wi-Fi. To set up an email account:

1. Touch the ⊚ icon. The Settings screen appears.
2. Touch **Mail, Contacts, Calendars**. The Mail, Contacts, Calendars settings appear, as shown in **Figure 8**.
3. Touch **Add Account…** A list of email services appears, as shown in **Figure 9**.
4. Select a service. The Information Entry screen (Gmail) appears, as shown in **Figure 10**. The appearance of the screen depends on the service that you selected. In **Figure 10**, Gmail is selected.
5. Touch each field to enter your email address, password, and username (all depending on your service). Your credentials are entered.
6. Touch **Next** at the top right of the Information Entry screen. The Account Settings screen appears, as shown in **Figure 11**.
7. Touch the ◯ switches next to the account services that you wish to turn on. The ◯ switches appear next to the selected services, and they are turned on.
8. Touch the button. Your email account is set up on your iPad.

Note: If you enter an incorrect user name or password, the following message appears: "The user name or password for >name of service here< is incorrect."

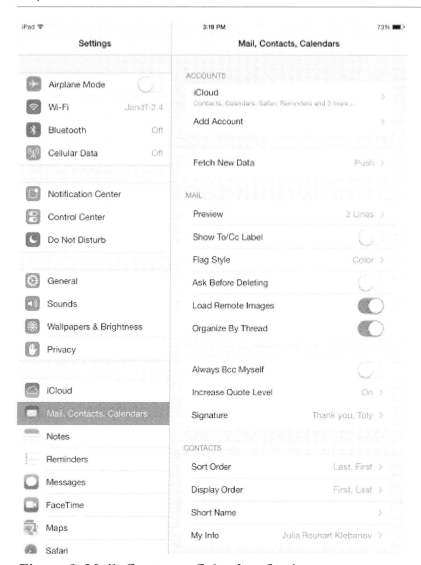

Figure 8: Mail, Contacts, Calendars Settings

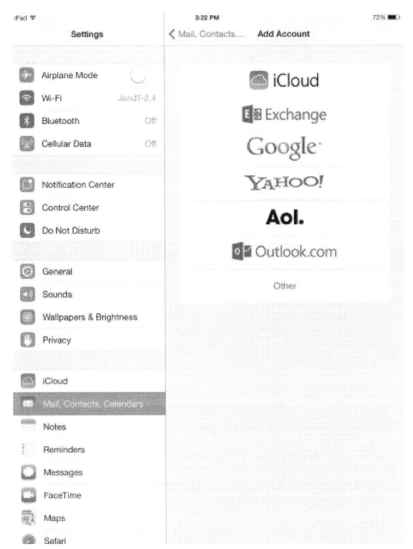

Figure 9: List of Email Services

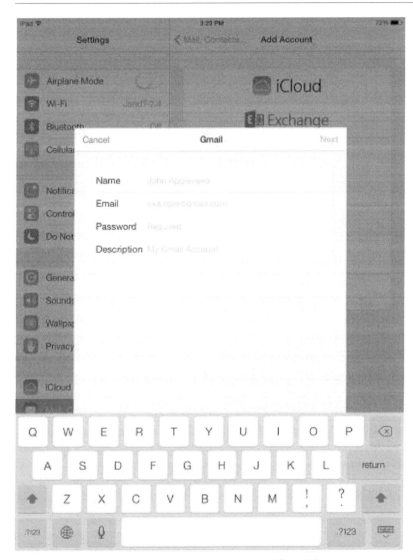

Figure 10: Information Entry Screen (Gmail)

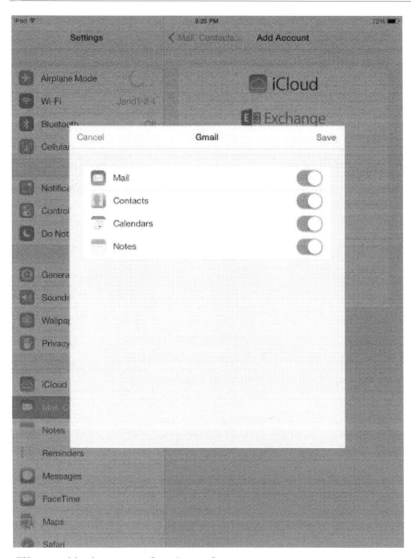

Figure 11: Account Settings Screen

6. Logging in to the Application Store

In order to buy applications, you will need to have an iTunes account. To set up a new iTunes account:

1. Touch the ⊚ icon. The Settings screen appears.
2. Scroll down and touch **iTunes & App Store**. The iTunes & App Store Settings screen appears, as shown in **Figure 12**. If you already have an Apple ID, enter your Apple ID and password and touch **Sign In**. Otherwise, proceed to step 3.
3. Touch **Create New Apple ID**. The New Account screen appears, as shown in **Figure 13**.
4. Touch the country where you live and touch **Done**. The country is selected.
5. Touch **Next** in the lower right-hand corner of the screen. The iTunes agreement screen appears.
6. Read the agreement and touch **Agree**. An acknowledgement dialog appears.
7. Touch **Agree**. The Account screen appears.
8. Touch each field and enter the required information. Touch **Next** in the bottom right-hand corner of the screen. The next Account Creation screen appears.
9. Touch each field and enter your credit card information. Touch **Next**. Your account is created.

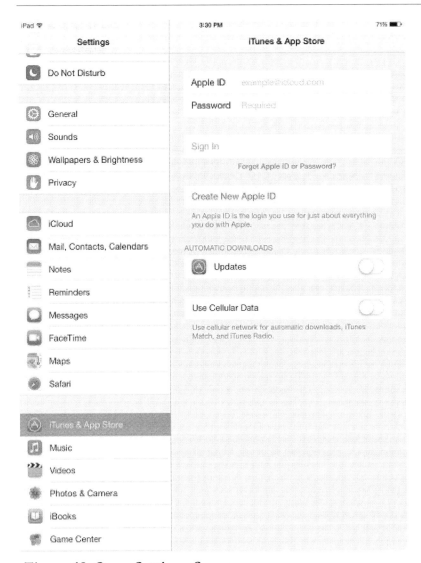

Figure 12: Store Settings Screen

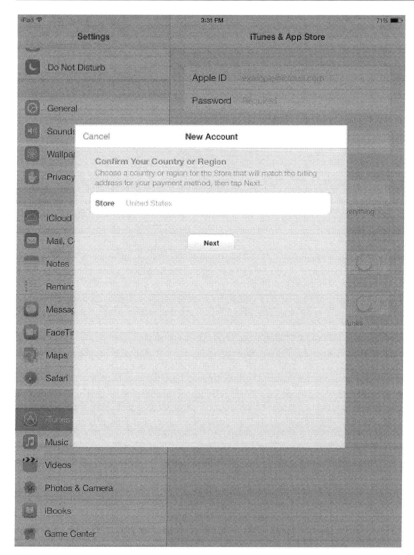

Figure 13: New Account Screen

7. Accessing Quick Settings through the Control Center

There are various settings that you can access without opening the Settings screen by using the Control Center. To use the Control Center:

1. Touch the bottom of the screen at any time and slide your finger up. The Control Center appears, as shown in **Figure 14**.
2. Touch one of the following icons at the top of the Control Center to turn on the corresponding function:

- Turns Airplane mode on or off.

- Turns Wi-Fi on or off.

- Turns Bluetooth on or off.

- Turns 'Do not disturb' on or off.

- Turns automatic screen rotation on or off.

- Turns the Mute function, which mutes all iPad sounds, on or off.

A white icon, such as a icon, indicates that the function is turned on.

3. Touch one of the following icons at the bottom of the Control Center to turn on the corresponding service:

- Opens the timer application.

- Turns on the camera.

Note: **Either** *the OR the icon will appear in the Control Center (but not both), depending on your Side Switch settings. Refer to* "Changing the Function of the Side Switch" *on page 229 to learn more about the side switch.*

Figure 14: Control Center

8. Using the Notification Center

The Notification Center shows event reminders and all types of alerts, such as calendar events, received texts, and missed calls. To open the notification center, touch the top of the screen at any time and move your finger down. The Notification Center opens, as shown in **Figure 15**. Touch a notification to open the corresponding application. For instance, touch a calendar event to open the calendar. You can also touch **All** or **Missed** at the top of the screen to view the corresponding notifications.

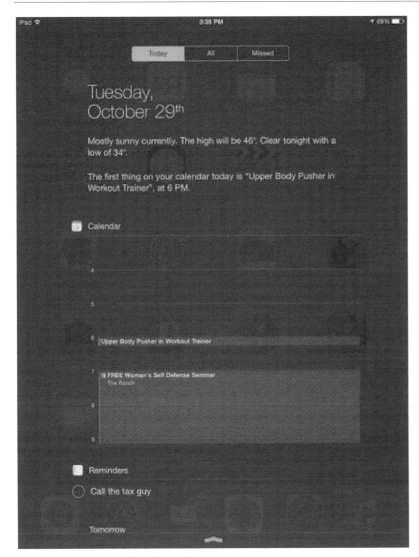

Figure 15: Notification Center

Managing Photos

Table of Contents

1. Taking a Picture

The iPad Air has a built-in five-megapixel rear-facing camera and a 1.2 megapixel front-facing camera. To take a picture, touch the ▢ icon. The camera turns on, as shown in **Figure 1**. Use the following tips when taking a picture:

- Touch the screen and slide your finger up to take a square picture. 'SQUARE' appears on the right side of the screen. Touch the screen again and slide your finger down to activate the default camera. 'PHOTO' appears on the right side of the screen.

- Touch the ▢ button in the upper right-hand corner of the screen at any time to use the front-facing camera.

- Touch the ◯ button to take a picture. The shutter closes and opens, and the picture is automatically stored in the 'Camera Roll' album.

Note: Refer to "Tips and Tricks" *on page 245 to learn how to take a picture directly from the Lock screen.*

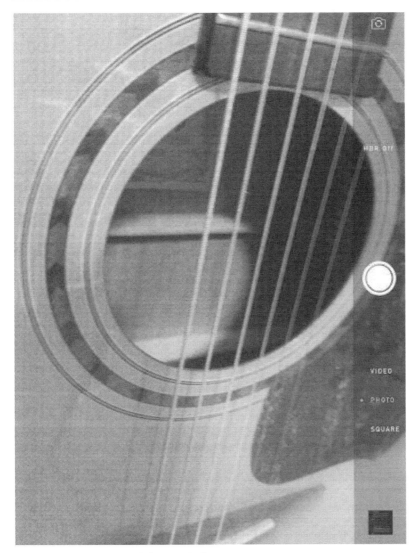

Figure 1: Camera Turned On

2. Browsing Photos

After taking pictures on your iPad or transferring them from your computer, you may view them at any time. To view saved photos:

1. Touch the ✻ icon on the Home screen. The Photos application opens.
2. Touch **Albums** at the bottom of the screen. A list of photo albums appears, as shown in **Figure 2**. The photos you have taken with the iPad are in an album called 'Camera Roll'.
3. Touch an album. The photos in the album appear, as shown in **Figure 3**.
4. Touch a photo. The photo appears in full screen.
5. Use the following tips when viewing photos:

   - Touch a photo with your thumb and forefinger and move the two fingers apart to zoom in on it. The zoom will center where your fingers were joined.
   - Touch the screen twice quickly to zoom out completely. Touch the photo with your thumb and forefinger spread apart and move the fingers together while touching the photo to zoom out gradually. Move your fingers apart to zoom in.
   - Touch the album name at the top left of the screen while viewing a photo to return to album view. If the album name is not shown, touch the photo once to make the photo menus appear at the top and bottom of the screen.
   - Touch the screen and slide your finger along the horizontal visual list of all photos and videos at the bottom of the screen. The iPad skims through the photos.

Figure 2: List of Photo Albums

Figure 3: Photos in an Album

3. Editing a Photo

The iPad provides basic photo-editing tools. To edit a photo:

1. Touch the ✿ icon at the Home screen. The Photos application opens.
2. Touch **Albums** at the bottom of the screen. A list of photo albums appears.
3. Touch an album. The photos in the album appear.
4. Touch a photo. The photo appears in full screen.

5. Touch **Edit** in the upper right-hand corner of the screen. The Photo Editing menu appears at the bottom of the screen, as shown in **Figure 4**.

6. Touch one of the following icons to edit the photo:

- Rotates the photo 90 degrees counter-clockwise. Touch repeatedly to keep rotating the photo. Touch **Save** in the upper right-hand corner of the screen to save the changes.

- Enhances the quality of the photo. Touch **Save** in the upper right-hand corner of the screen to save the changes.

- Adds a color effect, such as mono (grayscale) or instant (Polaroid) to the photo.

- Removes red-eye from the photo. Touch each red eye in the photo and then touch **Apply** in the upper right-hand corner of the screen. Touch **Save** in the upper right-hand corner to save the changes.

- Crops the photo. Touch the corners of the photo and drag the selected portion, as shown in **Figure 5**. Touch **Constrain** at the bottom of the screen and touch a size to choose a custom crop, and then touch **Crop** in the upper right-hand corner of the screen. Touch **Save** in the upper right-hand corner to save the changes.

Figure 4: Photo Editing Menu

Figure 5: Cropping a Photo

4. Deleting Photos

You may delete unwanted photos from your iPad to free up memory. To delete a photo:

Warning: Once a picture is deleted, there is no way to restore it. Deleting a picture removes it from all albums and Photo Stream.

1. Touch the ![icon] icon. The Photos application opens.
2. Touch **Albums** at the bottom of the screen. A list of photo albums appears.
3. Touch an album. The photos contained in the album appear.

4. Touch **Select** in the upper right-hand corner of the screen. 'Select Items' appears at the top of the screen.

5. Touch each photo that you wish to delete. A ✓ mark appears on each selected photo, as shown in **Figure 6**.

6. Touch the 🗑 button in the upper left-hand corner of the screen. A confirmation dialog appears.

7. Touch **Delete ## Photos**, where ## corresponds to the number of photos that you are deleting. The photos are deleted from all albums on the iPad, as well as Photo Stream, if they were backed up.

Figure 6: Selected Photos

5. Creating a Photo Album

You can create a photo album right on your iPad. To create a photo album:

1. Touch the ✿ icon. The Photos application opens.
2. Touch **Albums** at the bottom of the screen. A list of photo albums appears.

3. Touch the ✛ button in the upper left-hand corner of the screen. The New Album window appears, as shown in **Figure 7**.

4. Enter a name for the album and touch **Save**. The new photo album is created and you can now choose photos to add to it.
5. Touch a photo album and then touch photos to add them. Touch a photo a second time to deselect it. Touch **Albums** at the bottom of the screen at any time to return to the album list.
6. Touch **Done** in the upper right-hand corner of the screen. The selected photos are added to the new photo album.

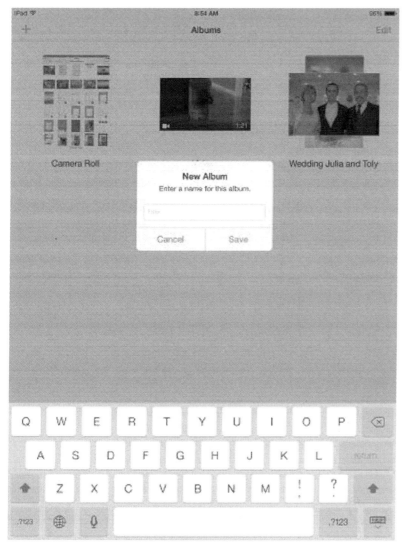

Figure 7: New Album Window

6. Editing a Photo Album

Photo albums stored on the iPad can be edited right from your device. Refer to *"Creating a Photo Album"* on page 37 to learn how to make a new photo album using your tablet.

To edit the name of a photo album:

1. Touch the ✳ icon. The Photos application opens.
2. Touch **Albums** at the bottom of the screen. A list of photo albums appears.
3. Touch **Edit** in the upper right-hand corner of the screen. The ⊗ buttons appear on the albums that may be edited.
4. Touch the name of a photo album. The virtual keyboard appears.
5. Enter a new name for the album and touch **Done**. The album is renamed.

To add photos to an album:

1. Touch the ✳ icon. The Photos application opens.
2. Touch **Albums** at the bottom of the screen. A list of photo albums appears.
3. Touch an album. The photos contained in the album appear.
4. Touch **Select** in the upper right-hand corner of the screen. Photos can now be selected.
5. Touch as many photos as you wish. The photos are selected and ✓ icons appear on the thumbnails.
6. Touch **Add To** at the bottom of the screen. A list of photo albums appears, as shown in **Figure 8**. You cannot add the photos to any album that is grayed out.
7. Touch the name of a photo album. The selected photos are added to the album.

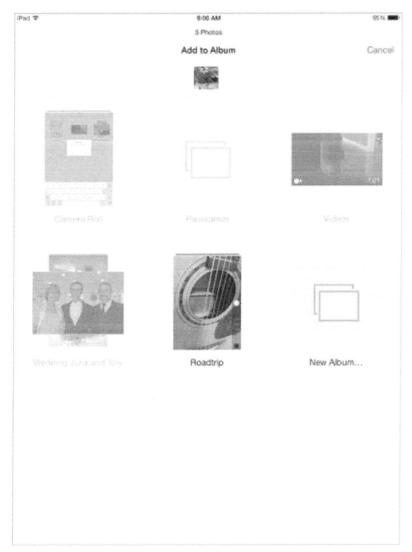

Figure 8: List of Photo Albums when Adding Photos

7. Deleting a Photo Album

Photo albums stored on the iPad can be deleted right from your tablet. To delete a photo album:

Warning: When an album is deleted from the iPad, any photos that are stored in other albums will remain on the iPad. Make sure any photos you wish to keep are stored in another album. Refer to "Editing a Photo Album" on page 39 to learn how to add photos to an album.

1. Touch the [icon] icon. The Photos application opens.
2. Touch **Albums** at the bottom of the screen. A list of photo albums appears.

3. Touch **Edit** in the upper right-hand corner of the screen. The ⊗ buttons appear on the albums that may be deleted.

4. Touch the ⊗ button next to an album. A confirmation dialog appears.

5. Touch **Delete Album**. The photo album is deleted.

8. Setting a Photo as the Wallpaper

You can set any photo stored on the iPad as the Home screen, Lock screen, or universal wallpaper. To set a picture as the wallpaper:

1. Touch the ❀ icon. The Photos application opens.

2. Touch **Albums** at the bottom of the screen. A list of photo albums appears.

3. Touch an album. The photos contained in the album appear.

4. Touch a photo. The photo appears in full screen.

5. Touch the ⬆ icon in the bottom left-hand corner of the screen. The Photo menu appears, as shown in **Figure 9**.

6. Touch **Use as Wallpaper** at the bottom of the screen. The Wallpaper menu appears, as shown in **Figure 10**.

7. Touch **Set Lock Screen**, **Set Home Screen**, or **Set Both**. The corresponding wallpaper is set to the selected photo.

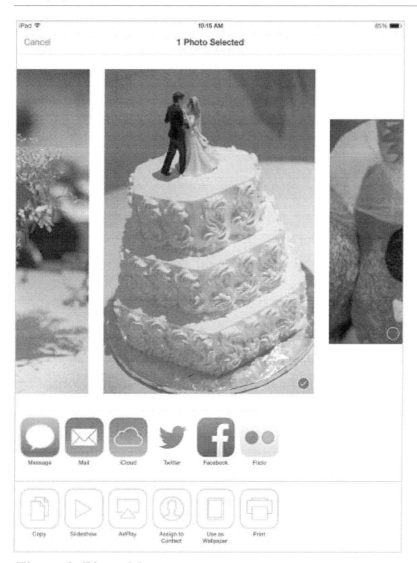

Figure 9: Photo Menu

Figure 10: Wallpaper Menu

9. Viewing a Slideshow

The iPad can play a slideshow using the photos in your albums. To begin a slideshow:

1. Touch the ![icon] icon. The Photos application opens.
2. Touch **Albums** at the bottom of the screen. A list of photo albums appears.
3. Touch an album. The photos in the album appear.
4. Touch **Slideshow** in the upper right-hand corner of the screen. The Slideshow Options appear, as shown in **Figure 11**.

5. Touch **Transitions** to customize the photo transitions. You can also add music to the slideshow by touching **Play Music**.

6. Touch **Start Slideshow** when ready. The slideshow begins. Touch anywhere on the screen to stop the slideshow at any time.

Figure 11: Slideshow Options

10. Importing and Exporting Pictures Using iPhoto

The only way to import or export photos from a computer to an iPad or vice versa is by using iPhoto on a Mac. It is not possible to import or export photos from a PC.
To import photos from the iPad into iPhoto on a Mac:

1. Connect the iPad to a Mac using the provided cable. iPhoto opens automatically. Click
   the ![icon] icon if iPhoto does not open. The iPad appears under 'Devices'. The screen shows
   any images that are on the iPad but not imported into iPhoto, as shown in **Figure 12**.
2. Click **Import All**. All images are imported.
3. Click one image at a time while holding the **Command Key** to import only selected
   images. Each image is selected and outlined in yellow. To deselect an image, click it again.
4. Click **Import Selected**. The photos are imported to your Mac and can be managed and
   edited in iPhoto.

Photos must be in an album to be exported. To create and export an album to the iPad:

1. Connect the iPad to a Mac using the provided cable. iPhoto opens automatically. Click
   the ![icon] icon if iPhoto does not open.
2. Click the ![button] button at the bottom left of the iPhoto window. The New Album window
   appears, as shown in **Figure 13**.
3. Type a name for the new album and click **Create**. The new album is created and appears
   on the computer screen.
4. Click an album to choose photos to move to the new album. The album opens.
5. Click photos while holding down the **Command Key** to select multiple images. Drag and
   drop the photos into the new album in the left pane. The photos are added to the new
   album. To select a single photo, click it.
6. Open iTunes on your Mac and click the iPad under the devices list. The contents of the
   iPad appear, as shown in **Figure 14**.
7. Click the **Photos** tab. The Photos tab appears, as shown in **Figure 15**.
8. Click the checkbox next to 'Sync photos'. Sync options are enabled.
9. Click the drop-down menu next to 'Sync photos from'. The Photo Sync drop-down menu
   appears, as shown in **Figure 16**.
10. Click **iPhoto**. The Sync folder is set to iPhoto.
11. Click **All Photos** to send all photo albums to the iPad or click **Selected Albums** to select a
    specific album. The photo albums are selected.
12. Click **Apply** at the bottom right of the iTunes window. The pictures from iPhoto are
    imported to the iPad.

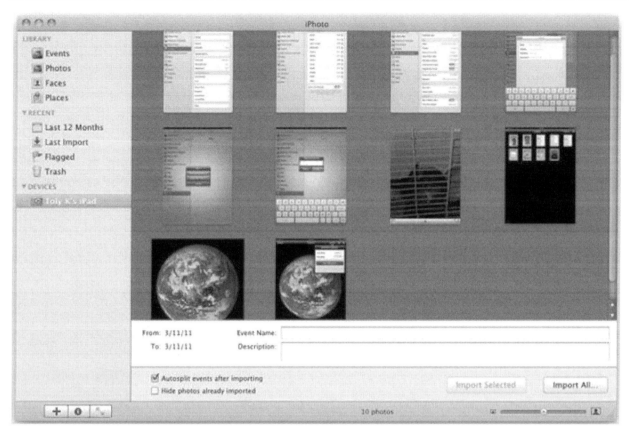

Figure 12: Unimported Photos on the iPad

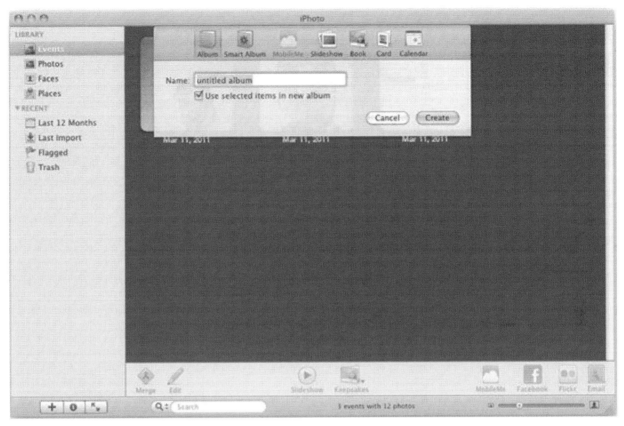

Figure 13: New Album Window

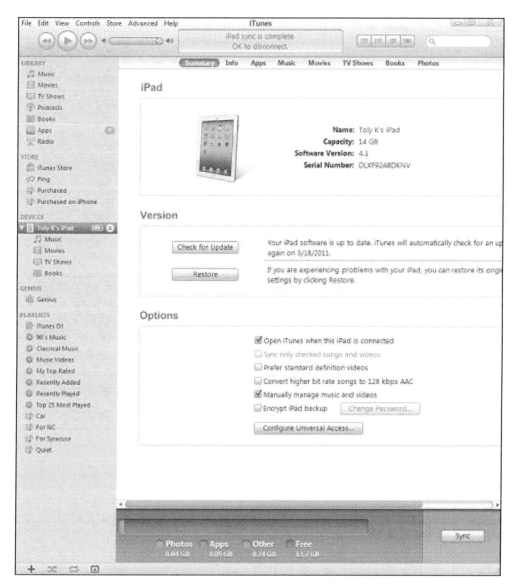

Figure 14: iPad Contents

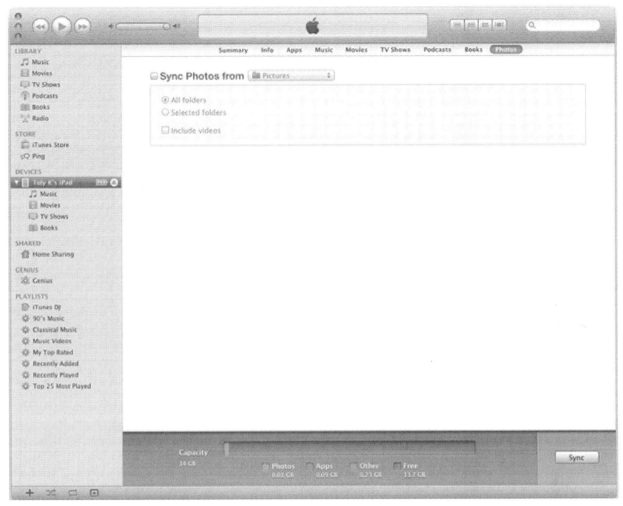

Figure 15: Photos on the iPad

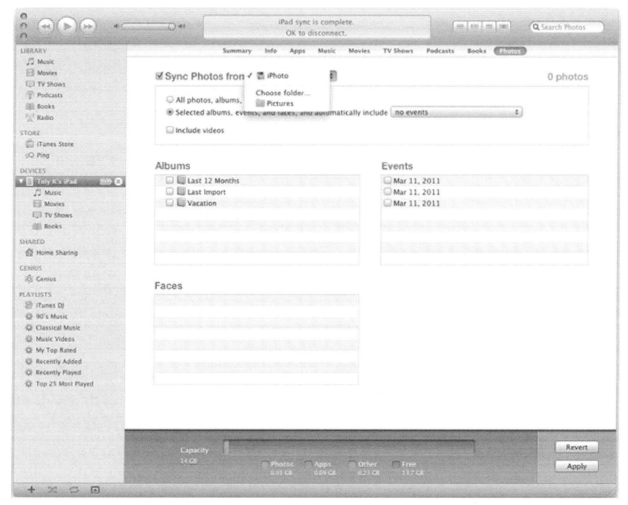

Figure 16: Photo Sync Drop-Down Menu

11. Importing and Exporting Pictures Using a PC

The iPad does not allow any photo management without the use of iPhoto on a Mac. To transfer photos from a PC to the iPad, email them to yourself. Save the attachments to the 'Saved Photos' album. The pictures emailed from the PC are now available on the iPad.

Managing Videos

Table of Contents

1. Capturing a Video

The iPad has a built-in camcorder that can shoot HD video. To capture a video on the iPad:

1. Touch the icon. The camera turns on.
2. Touch the screen and slide your finger down. 'VIDEO' appears on the right side of the screen, and the camcorder turns on, as shown in **Figure 1**.
3. Touch the button. The camera begins to record.
4. Touch the button. The camera stops recording and the video is automatically saved to the 'Moments' album.

Note: Touch the thumbnail in the bottom left-hand corner of the screen to preview the video.

Figure 1: Camcorder Turned On

2. Browsing and Trimming Stored Videos

You may browse and trim the videos that were captured on or transferred to your iPad.
To browse stored videos:

1. Touch the ✹ icon on the Home screen. The Photos application opens.
2. Touch **Albums** at the bottom of the screen. A list of photo albums appears, as shown in **Figure 2**. A 🎦 icon appears on every video in the album.
3. Touch a video in the list. The video opens.

4. Touch the ▶ icon. The video begins to play. Touch anywhere on the screen and then touch the ‖ button at any time to pause the video.

To trim a video:

1. Touch the 🌸 icon on the Home screen. The Photos application opens.
2. Touch **Albums** at the bottom of the screen. A list of photo albums appears. A 🎥 icon appears on every video in the album.
3. Touch a video in the list. The video opens and the

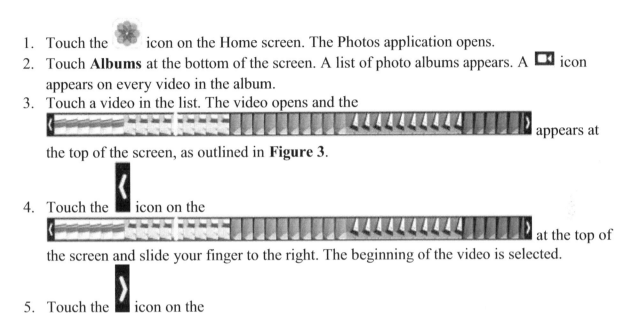

appears at the top of the screen, as outlined in **Figure 3**.

4. Touch the ◀ icon on the

at the top of the screen and slide your finger to the right. The beginning of the video is selected.

5. Touch the ▶ icon on the

at the top of the screen and slide your finger to the left. The end of the video is selected.

6. Touch **Trim** in the upper right-hand corner of the screen. The Trim menu appears, as shown in **Figure 4**.
7. Touch **Trim Original**, if you would like to overwrite the original video with the trimmed one. Otherwise, touch **Save as New Clip** to leave the original as it is and create a new video out of the trimmed one.

Figure 2: Video Open with Trim Bar at the Top

Figure 3: Trim Menu

3. Deleting Captured Videos

Delete videos to free up memory on the iPad. Only videos from the 'Saved Photos' and 'Camera Roll' albums may be erased directly from the iPad. Any video from an album that was created through iPhoto must be deleted using the same program. To delete videos from the iPad:

Warning: Once deleted, videos cannot be retrieved. Before deleting a video, be sure that you have backed it up or that you do not want it.

1. Touch the ✽ icon on the Home screen. The Photos application opens.
2. Touch **Albums** at the bottom of the screen. A list of photo albums appears.
3. Touch an album. The photos and videos contained in the album appear. A 🎥 icon appears on every video in the album.
4. Touch **Select** in the upper right-hand corner of the screen. 'Select Items' appears at the top of the screen.
5. Touch each video that you wish to delete. A ✓ mark appears on each selected video, as shown in **Figure 4**.
6. Touch the 🗑 button in the upper left-hand corner of the screen. A confirmation dialog appears.
7. Touch **Delete ## Videos**, where ## corresponds to the number of photos that you are deleting. The videos are deleted from all albums on the iPad, as well as Photo Stream, if they were backed up.

Figure 4: Selected Videos

4. Exporting Videos to the iPad Using iTunes

Videos may be transferred from your computer to your iPad via iTunes. To use iTunes to export videos to the iPad:

1. Download iTunes at **www.itunes.com/download**. Click **Download Now** and follow the on-screen instructions. iTunes is installed on the computer.
2. Open iTunes on your PC or Mac and connect the iPad to the computer using the provided USB cable. Unplug the USB end from the power adapter and plug that end into a USB port on your computer.

3. Turn on the iPad, if you have not already done so. The iPad appears under 'Devices' on the left side of the iTunes window.
4. Click **iPad**. The iPad summary appears on the right side of the screen, as shown in **Figure 5**.
5. Click the **Movies** tab. The current videos on the iPad and in your iTunes library appear, as shown in **Figure 6**.
6. Click as many videos as desired to select them for transfer. The videos are selected.
7. Click **Sync**. The selected videos are transferred to the iPad.

Note: When the transfer is complete, the following note appears at the top of the screen: "iPad sync is complete. OK to disconnect."

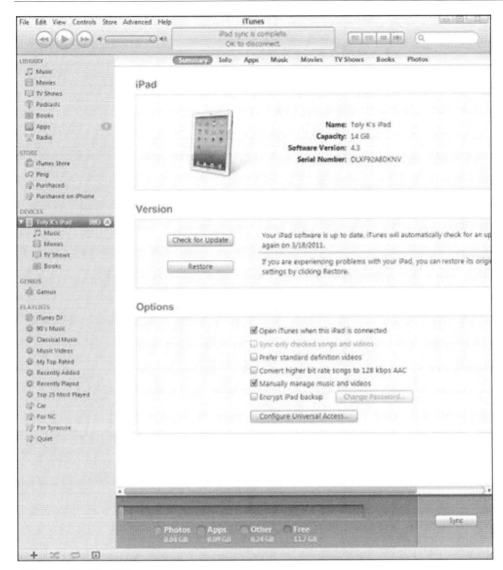

Figure 5: iPad Summary

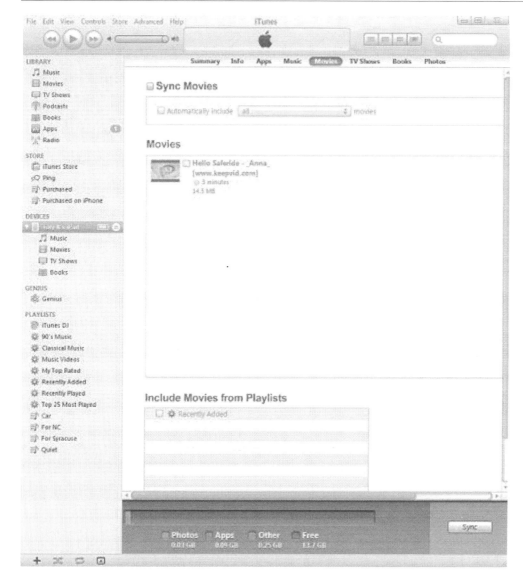

Figure 6: Videos on the iPad and in the iTunes Library

5. Viewing Downloaded Videos

The iPad can play downloaded videos. To view a downloaded video:

1. Touch the ![icon] icon. The Video Gallery appears, as shown in **Figure 7**.
2. Touch a video. The Video description appears.
3. Touch the ![button] button. The video begins to play.

4. Touch the screen anywhere. The Video Controls appear. The following controls may be available, depending on the video:

- Rewinds to the beginning of the scene or to the previous scene.

- Fast forwards to the next scene.

- Shows the video in Full-Screen mode. Some of the video will be cut off as a result.

- Shows all available languages. Some videos may be dubbed in languages other than English.

- Pauses the video at any time.

Figure 7: Video Gallery

Surfing the Web

Table of Contents

1. Navigating to a Website

You can surf the web using your iPad. To navigate to a website using the web address:

1. Touch the [icon] icon on the Home screen. The Safari Web browser opens.
2. Touch the Address bar at the top of the screen, as outlined in **Figure 1**. The keyboard appears. If you do not see the Address bar, touch the screen and move your finger down to scroll up.
3. Touch the [icon] button. The address field is erased.
4. Enter a web address and touch **Go**. Safari navigates to the website.
5. Touch the [icon] button. Safari navigates to the previous web page.
6. Touch the [icon] button. Safari navigates to the next web page.

Figure 1: Address Bar in Safari

2. Adding and Viewing Bookmarks

The iPad can store favorite websites as Bookmarks to allow you to access them faster in the future. To add a Bookmark in Safari:

1. Touch the ⬤ icon on the Home screen. The Safari browser opens.
2. Navigate to a website. Refer to *"Navigating to a Website"* on page 62 to learn how.

3. Touch the  button at the top of the screen. The Bookmark menu appears, as shown in **Figure 2**.
4. Touch **Bookmark**. The Add Bookmark window appears, as shown in **Figure 3**.
5. Enter a name for the bookmark and touch **Save** in the upper right-hand corner of the screen. The website is added to the Bookmarks.

Note: To view saved Bookmarks, touch the icon at the top of the screen in the Safari browser. The Bookmarks screen appears, as shown in **Figure 4**. *Touch a bookmark. Safari navigates to the indicated website.*

Figure 2: Bookmark Menu

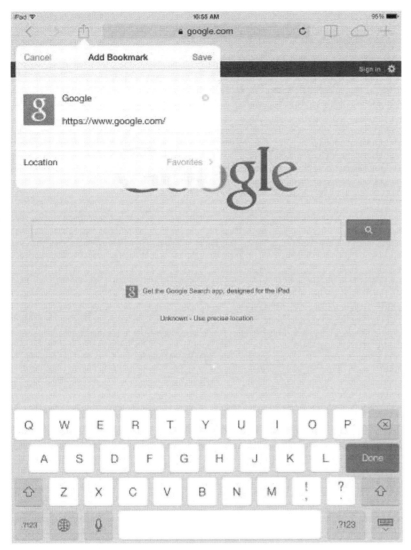

Figure 3: Add Bookmark Window

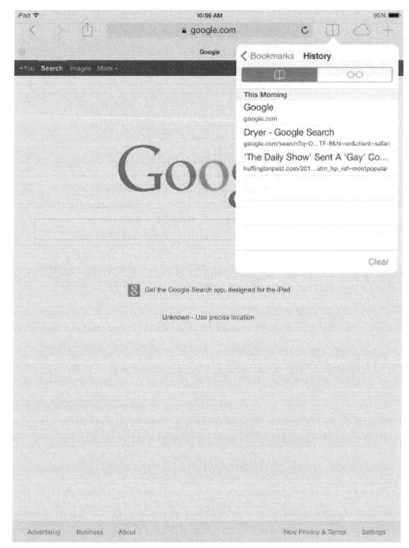

Figure 4: Bookmarks Screen

3. Adding a Bookmark to the Home Screen

On the iPad, bookmarks can be added to the Home screen; they will then appear like application icons. To add a bookmark to the Home screen as an icon:

1. Touch the ![icon] icon on the Home screen. The Safari browser opens.
2. Navigate to a website. Refer to **Navigating to a Website** to learn how.
3. Touch the ![button] button at the bottom of the screen. The Bookmark menu appears.

4. Touch **Add to Home Screen**. The Add to Home window appears, as shown in **Figure 5**.
5. Enter a name for the bookmark and touch **Add** in the upper right-hand corner of the window. The bookmark is added to the Home screen.

Figure 5: Add to Home Window

4. Managing Open Browser Tabs

The Safari Web browser supports up to nine open browser tabs, which are always visible at the top of the browser, as outlined in **Figure 6**. Use the following tips when working with browser windows:

- Touch a tab to open it.

- Touch the ┼ icon in the upper right-hand corner of the screen to open a new tab.

- Touch the ⊗ button at the top left of a tab to close it.

- Touch and hold a tab and drag it to the left or right to change its position.

Figure 6: Open Safari Tabs

5. Blocking Pop-Up Windows

Some websites may have pop-up windows that interfere with browsing the internet. To block pop-ups:

1. Touch the ⚙ icon on the Home screen. The Settings screen appears, as shown in **Figure 7**.
2. Scroll down and touch **Safari** on the left-hand side of the screen. The Safari Settings screen appears, as shown in **Figure 8**.
3. Touch the ⬜ switch next to 'Block Pop-Ups'. Pop-ups will now be blocked.
4. Touch the 🔵 switch next to 'Block Pop-Ups'. Pop-ups will now be allowed.

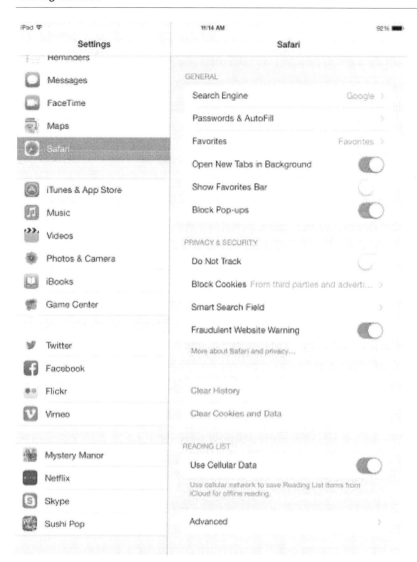

Figure 7: Settings Screen

Figure 8: Safari Settings Screen

6. Changing the Search Engine

Google, Yahoo, Bing, or Yandex can be set as the default search engine in Safari. When you get your new iPad, the default search engine is set to Google. Touch the address field at the top of the screen to use the search engine in Safari. To change the default search engine:

1. Touch the ⊚ icon on the Home screen. The Settings screen appears.
2. Touch **Safari**. The Safari Settings screen appears.
3. Touch **Search Engine**. A list of search engines appears.
4. Touch the preferred search engine. The default search engine is set.

7. Clearing the History, Cookies, and Cache

The iPad can clear the list of recently visited websites, known as the History, as well as other data, such as saved passwords, known as Cookies. The iPad can also delete data from previously visited websites, known as the Cache. To delete one or all of these items:

1. Touch the ⊚ icon on the Home screen. The Settings screen appears.
2. Touch **Safari**. The Safari Settings screen appears.
3. Touch **Clear History** or **Clear Cookies and Data**. A confirmation dialog appears.
4. Touch **Clear History** or **Clear Cookies and Data** again, depending on your selection in step 3. The selected data is deleted and the option is grayed out on the Safari Settings screen.

8. Viewing an Article in Reader Mode

The Safari browser can display certain news articles in Reader Mode, which allows you to read them like a book with no images or links. To view an article in Reader Mode, touch the ☰ button in the address bar at any time (when available), as outlined in **Figure 9**. Reader Mode turns on, as shown in **Figure 10**.

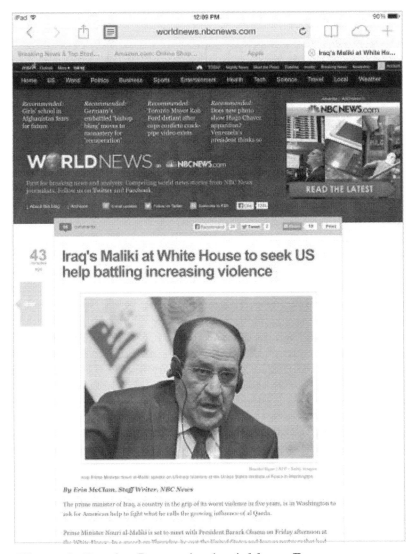

Figure 9: Reader Button in the Address Bar

Figure 10: Article in Reader Mode

9. Turning Private Browsing On or Off

In order to protect your privacy, the Safari Web browser allows you to surf the internet without saving the History or any other data showing that you have visited a particular website. To turn private browsing on or off:

1. Touch the ⚙️ icon on the Home screen. The Settings screen appears.
2. Touch **Safari**. The Safari Settings screen appears.
3. Touch the ⚪ switch next to 'Do Not Track'. Private browsing is turned on.
4. Touch the 🔘 switch next to 'Do Not Track'. Private browsing is turned off.

10. Setting Up the AutoFill Feature

Safari can automatically fill in personal information, such as passwords and credit card information, to save you time when filling forms or shopping online. To set up the AutoFill feature:

1. Touch the ⚙️ icon on the Home screen. The Settings screen appears.
2. Touch **Safari**. The Safari Settings screen appears.
3. Touch **Passwords & AutoFill**. The Passwords & Autofill screen appears, as shown in **Figure 11**.
4. Touch one of the following ⚪ switches turn on the corresponding AutoFill:

   - **Use Contact Info** - Enables the use of contact information when filling in forms. The Phonebook appears. Touch the name of a contact to use the contact information to fill in forms. It is recommended that you create a contact entry for yourself and use it for this feature.
   - **Names and Passwords** - Enables the use of saved names and passwords. You will be given the option to set up a security lock in order to keep your private information safe. Websites will give you the option to save your username and password. You can also touch the ⚪ switch next to 'Always Allow' to save passwords even for websites that will never save your password otherwise.
   - **Credit Cards** - Enables the use of saved credit card information. You will be given the option to set up a security lock in order to keep your private information safe. Touch **Saved Credit Cards**, and then touch **Add Credit Card** to add a new credit card.

Figure 11: Passwords & Autofill Screen

---

11. Customizing the Smart Search Field

The address bar in the Safari browser can act as a search field that assists you by matching your search terms while you type. To customize the smart search field:

1. Touch the ![icon] icon on the Home screen. The Settings screen appears.
2. Touch **Safari**. The Safari Settings screen appears.
3. Touch **Smart Search Field**. The Smart Search Field screen appears, as shown in **Figure 12**.

4. Touch one of the following 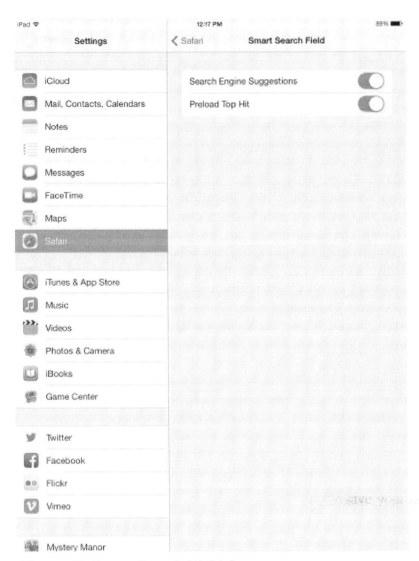 switches to turn on the corresponding Smart Search feature:

- **Search Suggestions -** Enables search term matching to assist you when performing a search.
- **Preload Top Hit** - Automatically loads the most popular search result when you perform a search. The web page is loaded in the background before you even touch the link.

Figure 12: Smart Search Field Screen

Using iTunes on the iPad

Table of Contents

1. Setting Up an iTunes Account

In order to buy content from the iTunes store, you will need to have an iTunes account. Refer to *"Logging in to the Application Store"* on page 22 to learn how to set one up.

2. Buying Music in iTunes

Music can be purchased directly from the iPad via iTunes. To buy music using the iTunes application:

1. Touch the ![icon] icon on the Home screen. The iTunes application opens.

2. Touch the ![icon] icon. The iTunes Music Store opens, as shown in **Figure 1**.

3. Touch **Featured**, **Charts**, or **Genres** at the top of the screen to browse music. The corresponding section appears.

4. Touch an album. The Album description appears, as shown in **Figure 2**.

5. Touch the price of the album. 'Buy Album' appears.

6. Touch **Buy Album**. The album is purchased. Touch the price of a song and then touch **Buy Song** to buy a single song.

7. Touch the ![icon] icon in the bottom right-hand corner of the screen. The Downloads screen appears, as shown in **Figure 3**. If the list is empty, all downloads are complete.

Note: You may need to enter your iTunes password when purchasing music on the iPad.

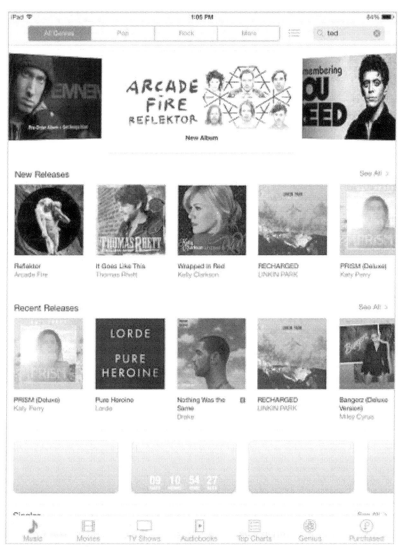

Figure 1: iTunes Music Store

Figure 2: Album Description

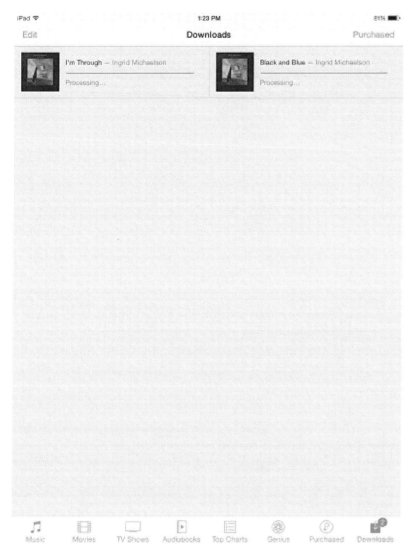

Figure 3: Downloads Screen

3. Buying or Renting Videos in iTunes

Videos can be purchased or rented directly from the iPad and viewed using the Music application. To buy videos using the iTunes application:

1. Touch the [icon] icon. The iTunes application opens.
2. Touch the [icon] icon or the [icon] icon at the bottom of the screen. The iTunes Video Store opens, as shown in **Figure 3** (Movie Store).
3. Touch a genre at the top of the screen to browse videos. Touch a video. The Video description appears, as shown in **Figure 4**.

4. Touch the price of the video. 'Buy Movie', 'Rent Movie', or 'Buy HD Episode' appears, depending on your selection.

5. Touch **Buy ...**, where '...' refers to the type of video that you are buying. The iPad may ask for your iTunes password. The video is purchased or rented and the download begins.

6. Touch the ⤓ icon in the bottom right-hand corner of the screen. The Downloads screen appears. If the list is empty, all downloads are complete.

Note: When renting a video, the video is available for 24 hours once you start watching it. Once 24 hours has passed, you will not be able to resume the video if you pause it.

Figure 4: iTunes Video Store (Movies)

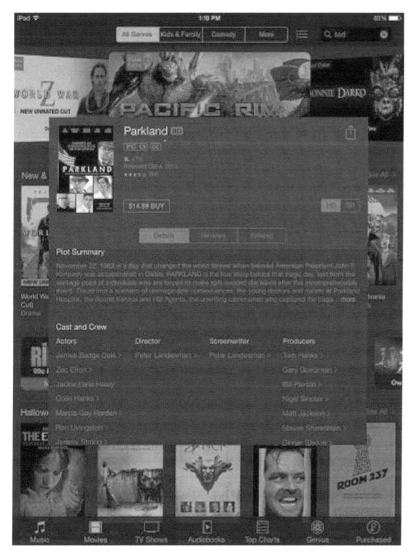

Figure 5: Video Description

4. Buying Tones in iTunes

Ringtones can be purchased directly from your iPad to use for incoming FaceTime calls. To buy ringtones using the iTunes application:

1. Touch the ⬚ icon. The iTunes application opens.
2. Touch **More** at the top of the screen. The More Options appear, as shown in **Figure 5**.
3. Touch **Tones** and then touch **All Tones**. The iTunes Tones Store opens, as shown in **Figure 6**.

4. Touch a genre at the top of the screen, or touch **All Genres** to browse ringtones. Touch a ringtone. A preview of the ringtone plays.
5. Touch the price of the ringtone. 'BUY TONE' appears.
6. Touch **BUY TONE**. The ringtone is purchased and downloaded to the iPad.
7. Touch the ⬇ icon in the bottom right-hand corner of the screen. The Downloads screen appears. If the list is empty, all downloads are complete.

To set the new ringtone as the default:

1. Touch the ⊚ icon on the Home screen. The Settings screen appears, as shown in **Figure 7**.
2. Touch **Sounds**. The Sound Settings screen appears, as shown in **Figure 8**.
3. Touch **Ringtone**. A list of ringtones appears.
4. Touch the recently downloaded ringtone. The ringtone is set as the default.

Note: Refer to "Assigning a Custom Ringtone to a Contact" on page 248 *to learn how to assign the new ringtone to a specific contact.*

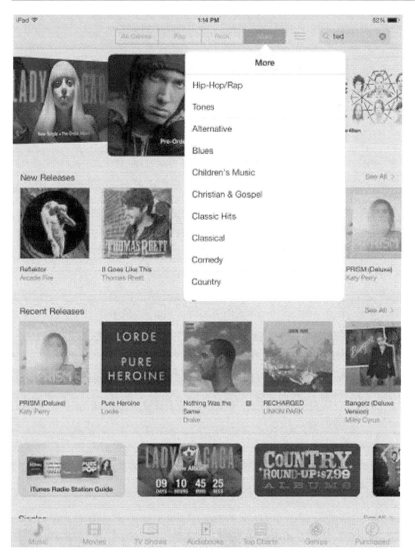

Figure 6: More Options

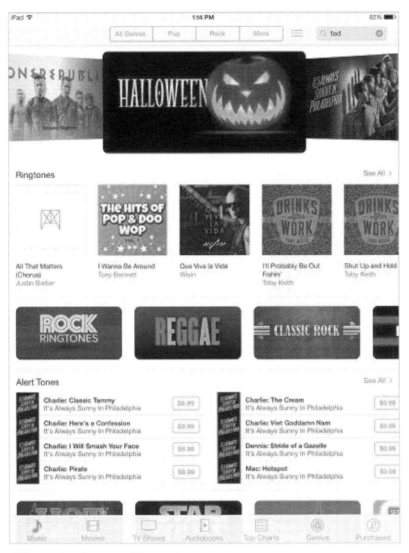

Figure 7: iTunes Tone Store

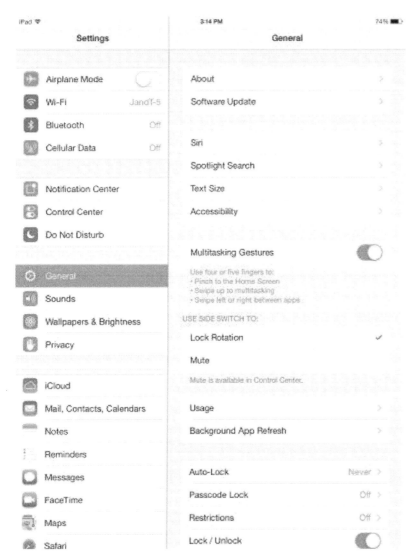

Figure 8: Settings Screen

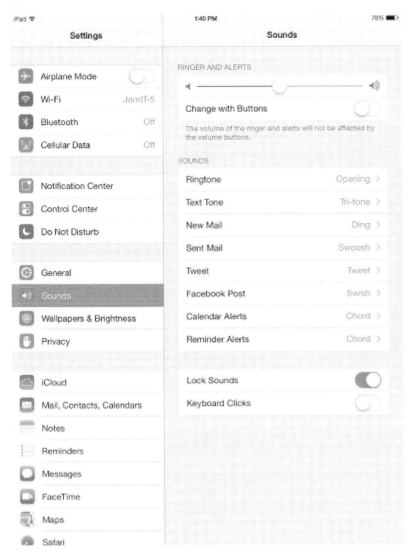

Figure 9: Sound Settings Screen

---

5. Searching for Media in iTunes

The iPad can search for any media in the iTunes Store. To search for media:

1. Touch the ![icon] icon. The iTunes application opens.
2. Touch the Search field in the upper right-hand corner of the screen. The virtual keyboard appears. Touch the ![button] button to clear the field, if necessary.
3. Enter the name of a song, video, or ringtone that you wish to find. Touch **Search** in the lower right-hand corner of the screen. The matching results appear, organized by the type of media, as shown in **Figure 9**.

4. Touch a song, video, or ringtone. The media description appears.

Note: Refer to "Buying Music in iTunes" *on page 79*, "Buying or Renting Videos in iTunes" *on page 82*, *or* "Buying Tones in iTunes" *on page 84 to learn how to purchase media.*

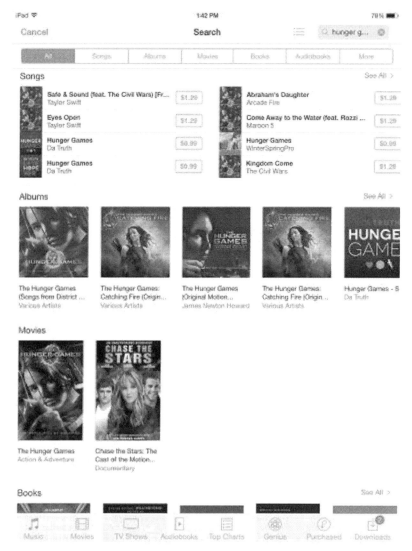

Figure 10: Available Media Results

6. Playing Media

To play media purchased in iTunes on the iPad, use the Music Application. To learn how, refer to *"Playing Music"* on the next page.

Playing Music

Table of Contents

1. Downloading Media

Use the iTunes Application to download media to the iPad. Refer to *"Using iTunes on the iPad"* on page 78 to learn how.

2. Playing Music

The Music application on the iPad can be used to play music. To listen to your music:

1. Touch the ![icon] icon. The Music application opens.
2. Touch one of the following icons at the bottom of the screen to browse music:

![icon] - Browse existing playlists.

![icon] - Browse existing artists.

![icon] - Browse existing songs.

○ ○ ○ - Browse existing albums, genres, compilations, or composers.

3. Use the following tips to navigate the Music Application:

- Touch a playlist, artist, or song to play the item. The item plays, as shown in **Figure 1**.
- After you have exited the Music application, touch the screen at the bottom and drag your finger up to bring up the music controls, as shown in **Figure 2**. Touch the name of the artist to return to the Music application. The music controls will also appear on the lock screen, as shown in **Figure 3**.

Figure 1: Music Playing

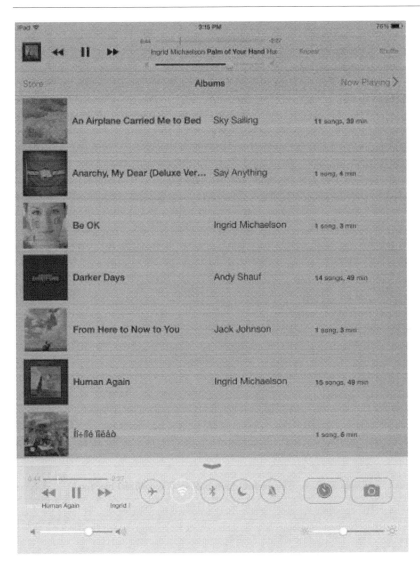

Figure 2: Music Controls

Figure 3: Music Controls on the Lock Screen

3. Using Additional Audio Controls

Use the Song Controls to control music while it is playing. Touch one of the following to perform the corresponding function:

◄◄ - Skip to the beginning of the current song or skip to the previous song.

►► - Skip to the next song.

II - Pause the current song.

▶ - Resume the current song when it is paused.

≔ - View the current playlist.

Repeat - Repeat the song or artist that is currently playing.

— | — - Drag the | on the bar at the top of the screen to go to a different part of the song.

Shuffle - Shuffle all songs in the playlist. Touch again to play the songs in order.

Create - Create an iTunes Radio station from the artist or song that is currently playing.

Note: Touch both **Repeat** *and* **Shuffle** *to play songs continuously in random order. To shuffle and play all songs on the iPad, go to the song list and touch* **Shuffle***.*

4. Creating a Playlist

Playlists can be created using the Music application. To create a playlist in the Music application:

1. Touch the 🎵 icon at the bottom of the screen in the Music application. The existing playlists appear, as shown in **Figure 4**.
2. Touch **New Playlist**. The New Playlist window appears, as shown in **Figure 5**.
3. Enter the name of the playlist and touch **Save**. A list of the songs on your iPad appears, as shown in **Figure 6**.
4. Touch one of the icons at the bottom of the screen to browse music to add to the new playlist. Refer to *"Playing Music"* on page 91 to learn more about finding music in the Music application.
5. Touch a song. The song is grayed out and added to the playlist.
6. Touch **Done** in the upper right-hand corner of the screen. The playlist is populated with the selected music.

After creating a playlist, you can add or remove music from it. To edit a playlist:

1. Touch the 🎵 icon in the Music application. The available playlists appear.
2. Touch a playlist. The Playlist screen appears.
3. Touch **Edit**. A ⊖ button appears next to every song in the playlist, as shown in **Figure 7**.
4. Touch the ⊖ button next to a song. 'Remove' appears next to the song.
5. Touch **Remove**. The song is removed from the playlist.

6. Touch the  button in the upper right-hand corner of the screen to add songs. To add songs, repeat steps 4 and 5 from the instructions above. The selected songs are added to the playlist.
7. Touch **Done**. The changes to the playlist are saved.

Note: Removing a song from a playlist will not delete it from the Music library.

Figure 4: Playlist Screen

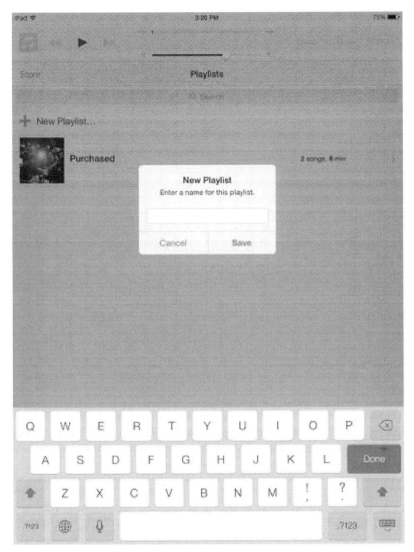

Figure 5: New Playlist Window

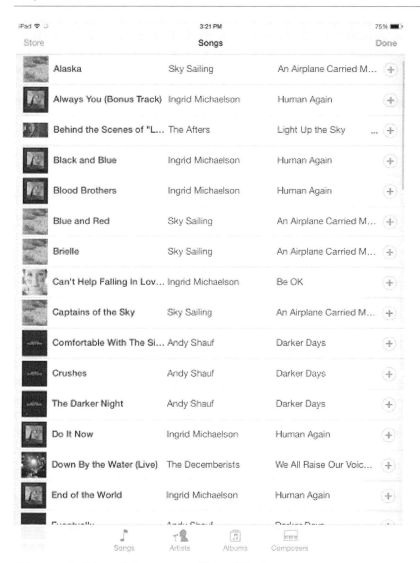

Figure 6: List of Songs on Your iPad

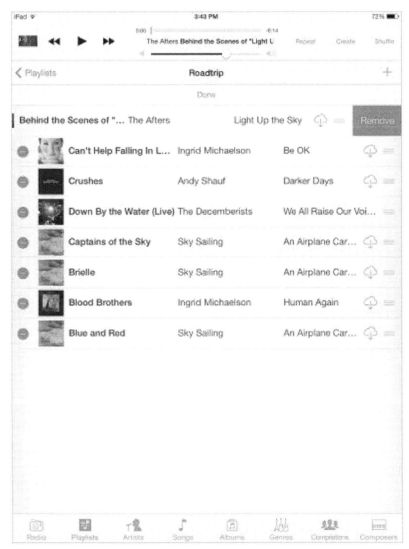

Figure 7: Playlist Editing Screen

5. Using the iTunes Radio

iOS 7 introduced the iTunes Radio, which is a free service that allows you to create personalized stations based on artists, songs, or genres.

To create a new iTunes Radio station:

1. Touch the 📻 icon at the bottom of the screen in the Music application. The iTunes Radio screen appears, as shown in **Figure 8**.

2. Touch the ✚ icon. The New Station screen appears, as shown in **Figure 9**.
3. Touch a genre in the list, or touch the search field at the top of the screen, and enter an artist, genre, or song. A preview of the station begins to play.

4. Touch the ⊕ icon next to the station name. The station is added to your stations.

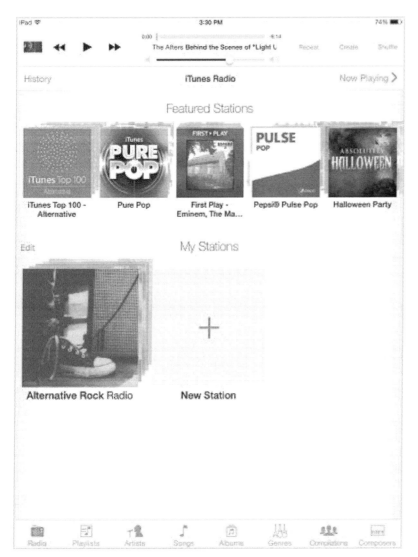

Figure 8: iTunes Radio Screen

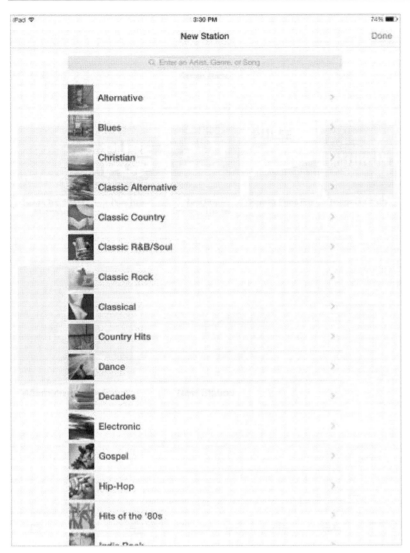

Figure 9: New Station Screen

Managing Email

Table of Contents

1. Setting Up the Email Application

Before the Email application can be used, at least one account must be set up on your iPad. Refer to *"Setting Up an Email Account"* on page 17 to learn how.

2. Reading Email

You can read your email on the iPad via the Email application. Before opening the Email application, make sure you have set up your email account. To read your email:

1. Touch the icon. The Email application opens and the Inbox appears, as shown in **Figure 1**. If the emails are not shown, touch **Inbox** in the upper left-hand corner of the screen if the name of your email is shown. This is the same name you gave the account when setting it up.
2. Touch an email. The email opens.

3. Touch **Inbox** in the upper left-hand corner of the screen in an email to return to the list of received emails. Touch **Mailboxes** in the upper left-hand corner of the Inbox to return to the list of mailboxes. The mailbox list varies depending on the mail service.

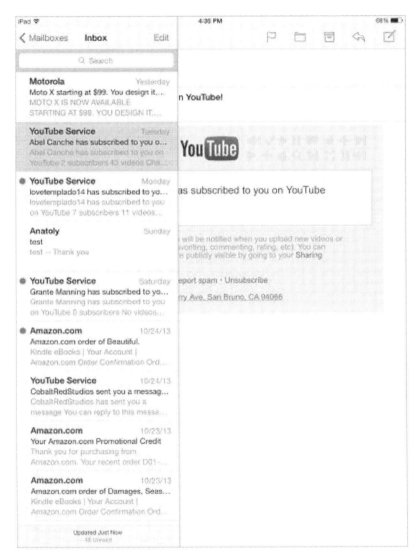

Figure 1: Email Inbox

3. Switching Accounts in the Email Application

If you have more than one active email account, you can switch between them or view all of your email in one Inbox. To switch to another account:

1. Touch the ![icon] icon. The Email application opens and your emails appear.
2. Touch **Mailboxes** in the upper left-hand corner of the screen while viewing a list of messages in a folder. A list of all active inboxes and accounts appears, as shown in **Figure 2**.
3. Touch an account. The Inbox associated with the selected account appears.

*Note: You can also touch **All Inboxes** to view all emails from the accounts attached to your iPad in a single joint folder.*

Figure 2: List of Active Inboxes and Accounts

4. Writing an Email

Compose email directly from the iPad using the Email application. To write an email while using the Email application:

1. Touch the ![button] button in the bottom right-hand corner of the screen. The New Email screen appears, as shown in **Figure 3**.
2. Start entering the name of a contact. A list of matching contacts appears below as you type.

3. Touch the name of the contact that you wish to email. The contact's email address is added to the addressee list. Alternatively, enter an email address from scratch. Enter as many additional addressees as desired.

4. Touch the text field to the right of 'Subject' and enter a topic for the message. The subject is entered.

5. Touch **return**. The cursor jumps to the body of the email.

6. Enter the content of the email and touch **Send** in the upper right-hand corner of the screen. The email is sent.

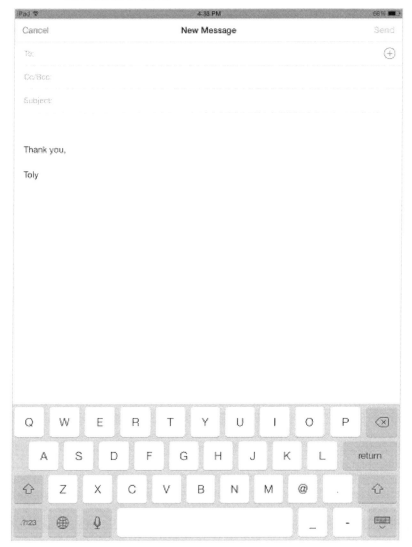

Figure 3: New Email Screen

5. Formatting Text

When writing an email on your iPad, you can format the text to add bold, italics, underline, or increase the quote level.

To add bold, italics, or underline text while writing an email:

- Touch and hold the text in the email that you wish to format. The Select menu appears above the text, as shown in **Figure 4**.
- Touch **Select All**. All of the text is selected. To select a single word, touch **Select**. Blue dots appear around the word or phrase.
- Touch and hold one of the blue dots and drag it in any direction. The text between the dots is highlighted and a Text menu appears, as shown in **Figure 5**.
- Touch the ![B I U] button. 'Bold', 'Italics', and 'Underline' appear. If you do not see ![B I U] button, touch the ![▶] button in the Text menu.
- Touch one of the formatting options. The associated formatting is applied to the selected text.

You can also increase the left margin, or quote level, in an email. To increase the quote level:

1. Touch and hold any location in your email. The text cursor flashes in the selected location.
2. Touch **Quote Level**. The Quote Level options appear.
3. Touch **Decrease** or **Increase** to adjust the Quote Level accordingly. The new Quote Level is set and applied to the paragraph where the text cursor is currently flashing.

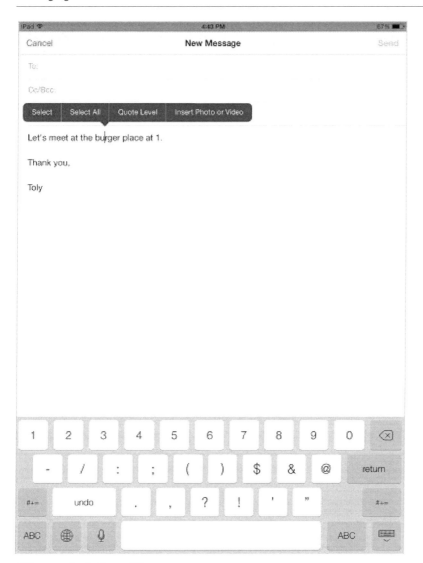

Figure 4: Select Menu

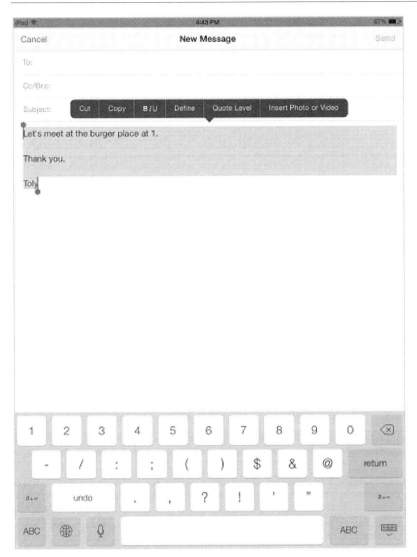

Figure 5: Text Menu

6. Replying to and Forwarding Email Messages

After receiving an email, you can reply to the sender or forward the email to a new recipient. To reply to, or forward, an email:

1. Touch the ⊠ icon. The Email application opens.
2. Touch an email. The email appears.
3. Touch the ↰ button at the top of the screen. The Reply menu appears, as shown in **Figure 6**.
4. Touch **Reply** to reply to the message or touch **Forward** to forward the message. The New Message screen appears. The subject at the top is preceded by 'Re:' if replying or 'Fwd:' if forwarding. The original email is copied in the body. If replying, the addressee field is filled in.
5. Touch the text field next to 'To:' and enter an addressee, if necessary. The addressee is entered.
6. Touch the text field to the right of 'Subject' to enter a different subject for your message, if desired. The subject is entered.
7. Touch the text field below 'Subject' and enter a message, if desired. The message is entered.
8. Touch **Send** in the upper right-hand corner of the screen. The email is sent.

Note: When forwarding, the attachment menu will appear if the original message has an attachment. Touch **Include** *if you wish to include the attachment when you forward the email. Otherwise, touch* **Don't Include***.*

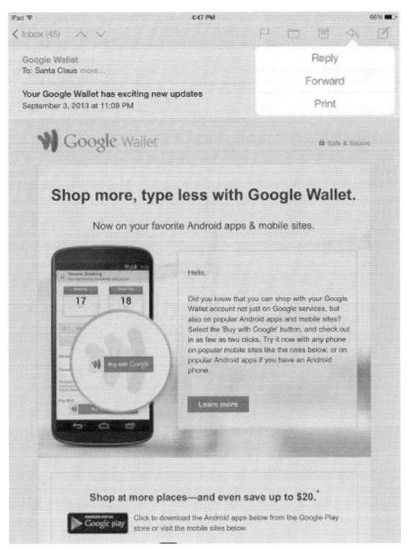

Figure 6: Reply Menu

7. Attaching a Picture or Video to an Email

While composing an email, you may wish to attach a picture or video to send to the recipient. To attach a picture or video to an email:

1. Touch and hold anywhere in the content of the email. The Select menu appears above the text.

2. Touch the ▶ button in the Select menu, and then touch **Insert Photo or Video**. A list of photo albums stored on your iPad appears, as shown in **Figure 7**.

3. Touch the photo album that contains the photo that you wish to attach. The photo album opens and a list of photo thumbnails appears, as shown in **Figure 8**.

4. Touch the photo that you wish to attach. A preview of the photo appears.

5. Touch **Choose**. The selected photo is attached. Alternatively, touch **Cancel** to return to the list of photos.

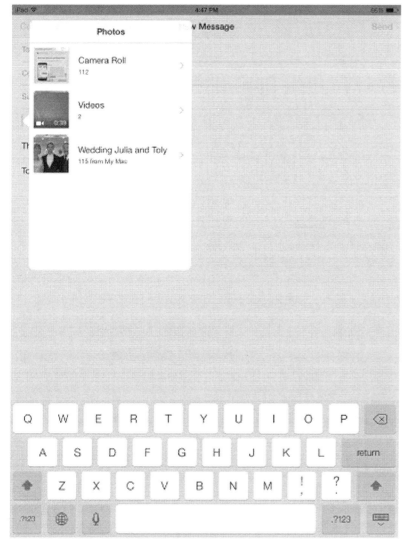

Figure 7: List of Photo Albums

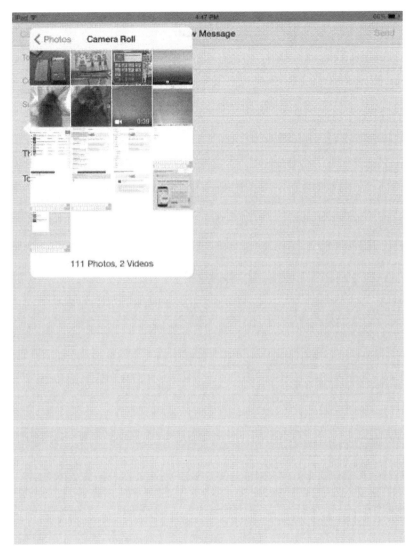

Figure 8: List of Photo Thumbnails

8. Moving an Email in the Inbox to Another Folder

You may wish to organize emails into folders so that you can find them more easily. To move an email in the Inbox to another folder:

1. Touch an email in the Inbox. The email opens.

2. Touch the ⬜ button at the top of the screen. A list of available folders appears, as shown in **Figure 9**.

3. Touch the name of a folder. The selected email is moved to the folder. To view a list of your folders, touch **Mailboxes** in the upper left-hand corner of the screen while viewing the Inbox.

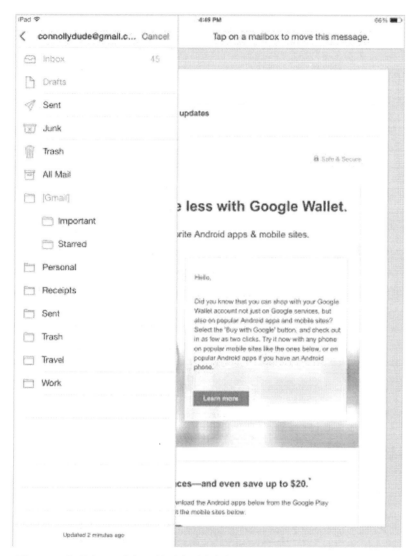

Figure 9: List of Available Folders

9. Flagging an Important Email

You may flag emails that are of the greatest importance in order to find them more quickly. This feature is especially useful if you do not have the time to read the email immediately, and wish to return to it in the near future. To flag an important email:

1. Touch an email in the Inbox. The email opens.

2. Touch the ⚑ button at the bottom of the screen. The Flagging menu appears, as shown in **Figure 10**.

3. Touch **Flag**. The email is flagged as 'Important'. You may also touch **Mark as Unread** to flag the email so that you remember to read it later, or **Move to Junk** to mark the email as spam (options may vary based on email service).

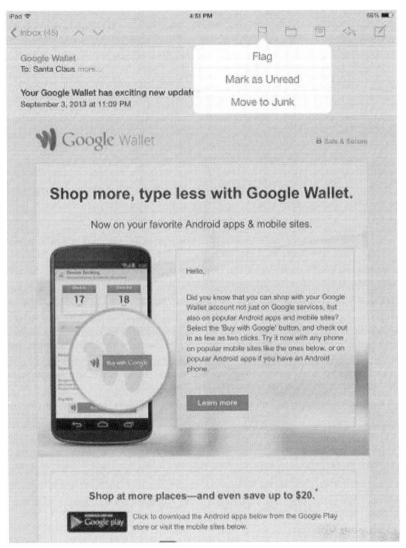

Figure 10: Flagging Menu

10. Archiving Emails

You may archive emails from your Inbox to free up space and improve organization. Archiving emails moves them to a folder that does not take up space on your iPad. Therefore, you never need to delete an email, and can always recover it if you did not mean to delete it. You may archive as many emails as you like. To archive an email:

1. Touch the ⊠ icon. The email application opens.
2. Touch and hold an email in the list and drag your finger to the left. 'Archive' appears to the right of the email.
3. Touch **Archive**. The email is sent to the Archive folder and disappears from the Inbox.

   You can also archive an email by touching the ⬓ icon at the top of the screen while viewing an open email.

*Note: Touch **Mailboxes** in the upper left-hand corner of the screen and then touch **All Mail** to view all emails, including those that have been archived.*

11. Changing the Default Signature

The iPad can set a default signature that will be attached to the end of each email that is sent from the iPad. To set or change this signature:

1. Touch the ⚙ icon. The Settings screen appears, as shown in **Figure 11**.
2. Touch **Mail, Contacts, Calendars** at the bottom of the screen. The Mail, Contacts, Calendars screen appears, as shown in **Figure 12**.
3. Scroll down and touch **Signature**. The Signature screen appears, as shown in **Figure 13**.
4. Enter a signature and touch **Mail...** in the upper left-hand corner of the screen when finished. The new signature is saved.

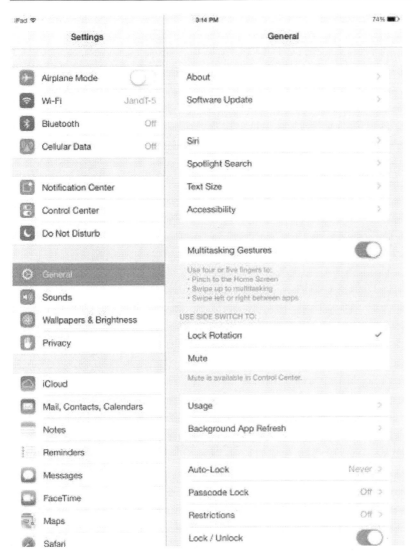

Figure 11: Settings Screen

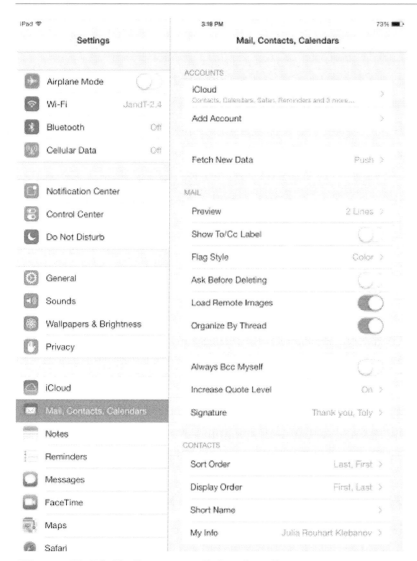

Figure 12: Mail, Contacts, Calendars Screen

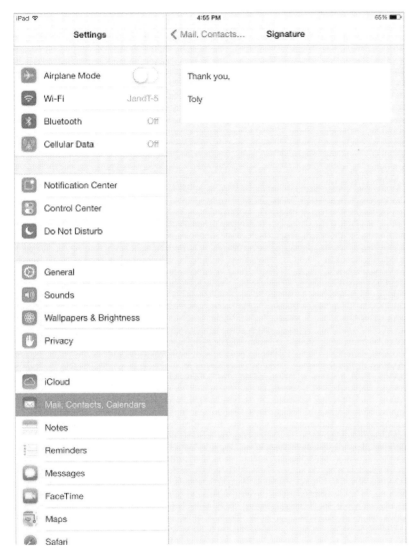

Figure 13: Signature Screen

12. Changing How You Receive Email

There are two options for receiving email on the iPad. The iPad can check for new email only when you refresh the Inbox, or it can constantly check for email and display an alert when a new email arrives. To set the iPad to either check for email at regular intervals or only when you refresh the Inbox:

1. Touch the ⚙ icon. The Settings screen appears.
2. Touch **Mail, Contacts, Calendars** at the bottom of the screen. The Mail, Contacts, Calendars screen appears.

3. Touch **Fetch New Data**. The Fetch New Data screen appears, as shown in **Figure 14**.

4. Touch the ⬭ switch next to 'Push'. Push is turned on, and the Email application will constantly check for new email and alert you when a new one arrives.

5. Touch the ⬬ switch next to 'Push'. Push is turned off, and the Email application will only check for new email when you touch the top of the Inbox and slide your finger down to refresh it.

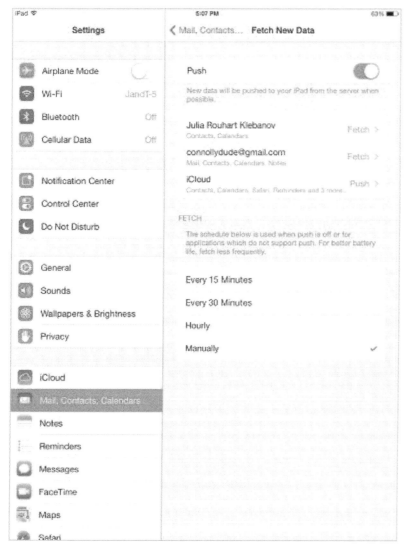

Figure 14: Fetch New Data Screen

13. Changing Email Options

There are various options that change the way your Email application works. Touch the ⊚ icon and then touch **Mail, Contacts, Calendars** to change one of the following options:

- **Preview** - Choose the number of lines of an email message to preview in the Inbox.
- **Show To/Cc Label** - Choose whether to hide the 'To' and 'Cc' labels and show only addresses.
- **Flag Style** - Choose the type of shape to use (color or shape) when flagging an email.
- **Ask Before Deleting** - Choose whether to display a confirmation before deleting an email.
- **Load Remote Images** - Choose whether to load images in an email automatically.
- **Organize by Thread** - Choose whether to group all emails with the same contact as a conversation.
- **Always Bcc Myself** - Choose whether the email application sends a copy of each email to your own email address for your records.
- **Increase Quote Level** - Choose whether to increase the left margin when replying to or forwarding an email.

Managing Contacts

Table of Contents

1. Adding a New Contact

The iPad can store phone numbers, email addresses, and other Contact Information in its Phonebook. To add a new contact to the Phonebook:

1. Touch the ![icon] icon on the Home screen. The Address Book appears, as shown in **Figure 1**.

2. Touch the ✛ button at the top of the screen. The New Contact screen appears, as shown in **Figure 2**.

3. Touch **First**. The keyboard appears. Enter the first name of the contact.

4. Touch **Last**. Enter the last name of the contact.

5. Touch **add phone**. The keypad appears. Enter the contact's phone number. The number is entered.

6. Touch any empty field to enter the desired information, and then touch **Done** in the upper right-hand corner of the screen. The contact's information is stored.

Note: Refer to "Tips and Tricks" *on page 245 to learn how to add an extension after the contact's phone number.*

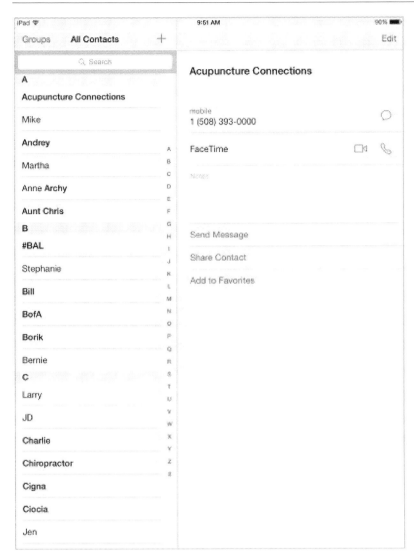

Figure 1: Address Book

Figure 2: New Contact Screen

2. Finding a Contact

After adding contacts to your iPad's Phonebook, you may search for them. To find a stored contact:

1. Touch the ![icon] icon on the Home screen. The Phonebook appears.
2. Touch **Search** at the top of the screen. The keyboard appears.
3. Start typing the name of a contact. Contact matches appear as you type, as shown in **Figure 3**.

4. Touch a match. The Contact Info screen appears, as shown in **Figure 4**.

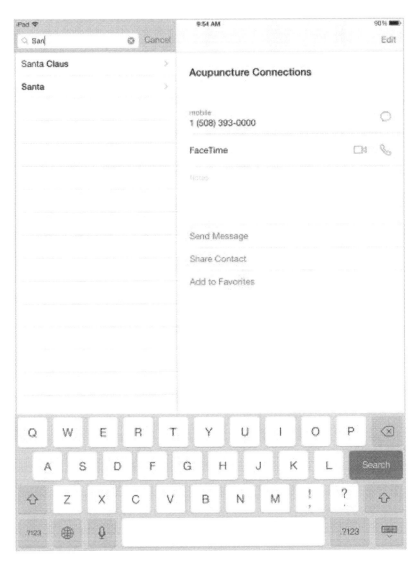

Figure 3: Contact Matches

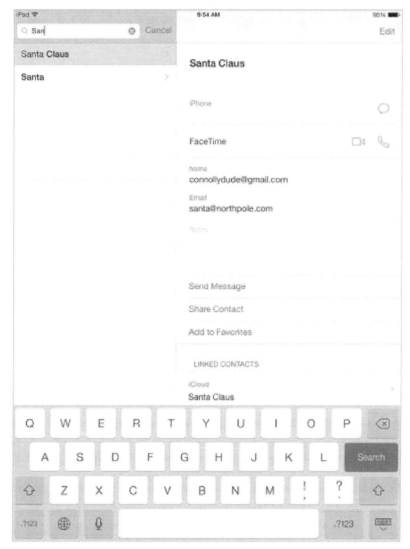

Figure 4: Contact Info Screen

3. Deleting a Contact

You may delete contact information from your Phonebook in order to free up space or for organizational purposes. To delete unwanted contact information:

Warning: There is no way to restore contact information after it has been deleted.

1. Touch the ![icon] icon on the Home screen. The Phonebook appears.
2. Find and touch the name of the contact that you wish to delete. The Contact Info screen appears. Refer to *"Finding a Contact"* on page 124 to learn how to search for a contact.

3. Touch **Edit** in the upper right-hand corner of the screen. The Contact Information Editing screen appears.

4. Touch **Delete Contact** at the bottom of the screen, as outlined in **Figure 5**. A Confirmation menu appears.

5. Touch **Delete Contact** again. The contact's information is deleted and will no longer appear in your Phonebook.

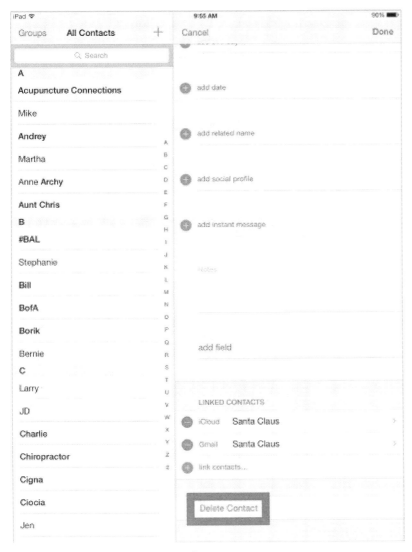

Figure 5: Delete Contact Screen

4. Editing Contact Information

After adding contacts to your Phonebook, you may edit them at any time. To edit an existing contact's information:

1. Touch the ![icon] icon on the Home screen. The Phonebook appears. If a list of all contacts does not appear, touch **All Contacts** in the upper left-hand corner of the screen to view the list.
2. Find and touch a contact's name. The Contact Info screen appears. Refer to *"Finding a Contact"* on page 124 to learn how to search for a contact.
3. Touch **Edit** in the upper right-hand corner of the screen. The Contact Editing screen appears.
4. Touch a field to edit the corresponding information. Touch **Done** in the upper right-hand corner of the screen. The contact's information is updated.

5. Sharing a Contact's Information

To share a contact's information with someone else:

1. Touch the ![icon] icon. The Phonebook appears.
2. Find and touch a contact's name. The Contact Info screen appears. Refer to *"Finding a Contact"* on page 124 to learn how.
3. Touch **Share Contact** at the bottom of the screen. The Sharing Options menu appears, as shown in **Figure 6**.
4. Follow the steps in the appropriate section below to learn how to email or text the contact's information.

To send the contact's information via email:

- Touch the ![icon] icon in the Sharing Options menu. The New Email screen appears, as shown in **Figure 7**. Choose one of the following options for entering the email address:
    - Start typing the name of the contact with whom you wish to share the information. The matching contacts appear. Touch the contact's name. The contact's email address is added.
    - Enter the email address from scratch. To use a number, touch _123 at the bottom left of the screen. When done, touch the **return** button in the lower right-hand corner of the screen. Enter more addresses if needed.

- Touch the ⊕ icon to select as many contacts from your Phonebook, or enter as many email addresses as you wish.

- Enter an optional subject by touching **Subject**, and touch **CC** to add other addresses to which to send the information.
- Touch **Send** in the upper right-hand corner of the screen. The contact's information is sent to the selected email addresses.

To send a contact's information via multimedia message, touch the ◯ icon in the Sharing Options menu. The New Message screen appears, as shown in **Figure 8**. Enter an iMessage email address or phone number and touch **Send**. The contact's information is sent. There are three methods for entering the email address or phone number:

- Start typing the name of the contact with whom you wish to share the information. Matching contacts appear. Touch the contact's name. The contact's number is added.

- Type the phone number or email address from scratch. To use numbers, touch the 123 button at the bottom left of the screen. When done, touch the return button in the lower right-hand corner of the screen.

- Touch the ⊕ icon to select one or more contacts from the Phonebook.

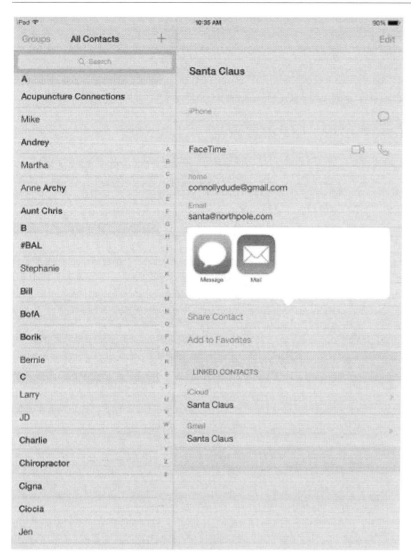

Figure 6: Sharing Options Menu

Figure 7: New Email Screen

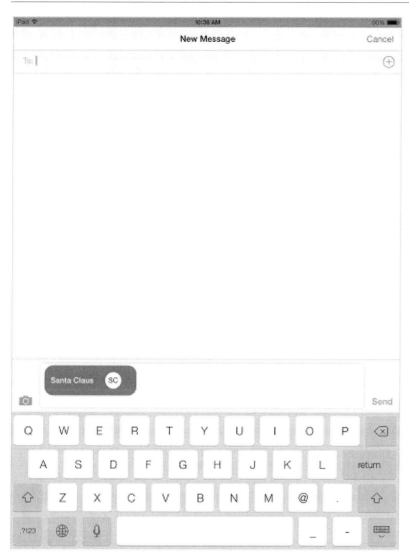

Figure 8: New Message Screen

Managing Applications

Table of Contents

1. Setting Up an iTunes Account

In order to buy applications, you will need to have an iTunes account. Refer to *"Logging in to the Application Store"* on page 22 to learn how to set up a new iTunes account.

2. Signing In to a Different iTunes Account

If more than one person uses your iPad, you may wish to sign in with an alternate Apple ID. Only one Apple ID may be signed in at a time. To sign out and sign in to a different iTunes account:

1.   Touch the ⚙ icon. The Settings screen appears, as shown in **Figure 1**.
2.   Scroll down and touch **iTunes & App Store**. The iTunes & App Store Settings screen appears, as shown in **Figure 2**. If someone is signed in to their iTunes account on the iPad, their email appears at the top of the screen.

3. Touch the email address at the top of the screen. The Apple ID window appears, as shown in **Figure 3**.
4. Touch **Sign Out**. The account is signed out.
5. Touch **Apple ID**. The virtual keyboard appears.
6. Enter your registered email address and password. Refer to **Setting Up an iTunes Account** to learn how to create a new iTunes account.
7. Touch **Sign In**. The account is signed in and the owner's email is shown at the top of the iTunes & App Store screen.

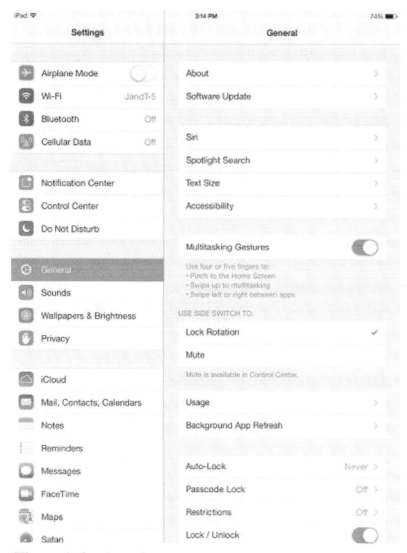

Figure 1: Settings Screen

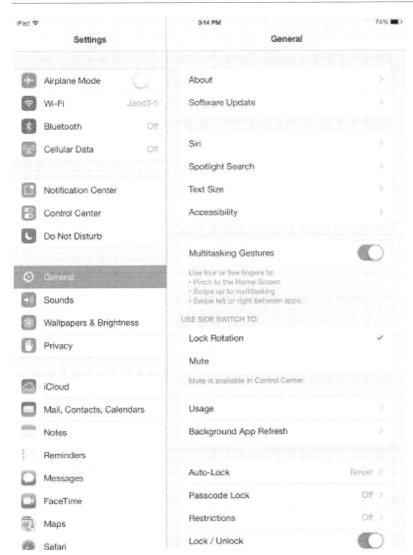

Figure 2: iTunes & App Store Settings Screen

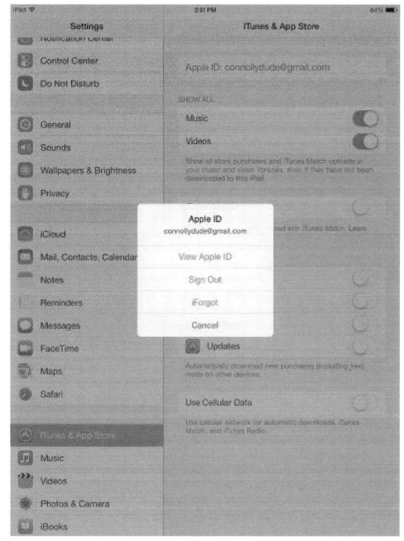

Figure 3: Apple ID Window

3. Editing iTunes Account Information

You must keep your account information up to date in order to purchase applications from the iTunes Application Store. For instance, when your billing address changes or your credit card expires, you must change your information. To edit iTunes account information:

1. Touch the icon. The Settings screen appears.
2. Scroll down and touch **iTunes & App Store**. The iTunes & App Store Settings screen appears. If someone is signed in to their iTunes account on the iPad, their email appears at the top of the screen.

3. Touch **Sign In** and **Use Existing Apple ID** if you are not signed in. Enter your registered email and password and touch **OK**. You are signed in.
4. Touch your email at the top of the screen. The Apple ID window appears.
5. Touch **View Apple ID**. The Account Screen appears with your personal account information, as shown in **Figure 4**.
6. Touch a field to edit it, and then touch **Done** in the upper right-hand corner of the screen. The new information is saved.

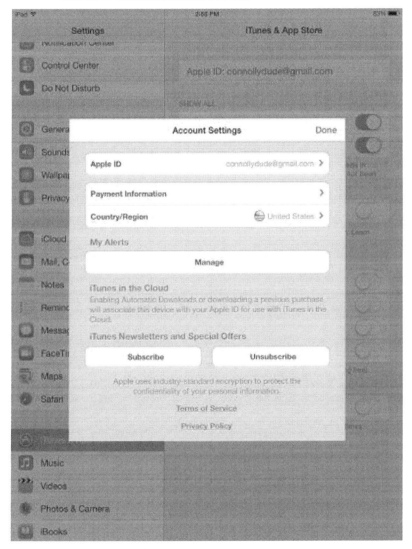

Figure 4: Account Screen

4. Searching for an Application to Purchase

Use the Application Store to search for applications. There are three ways to search for applications:

Manual Search

To search for an application manually:

1. Touch the ⒶＡ icon. The Application Store opens, as shown in **Figure 5**.
2. Touch the 🔍 button at the top of the screen. The virtual keyboard appears at the bottom of the screen.
3. Enter the name of an application and touch **Search**. A list of matching results appears, as shown in **Figure 6**.

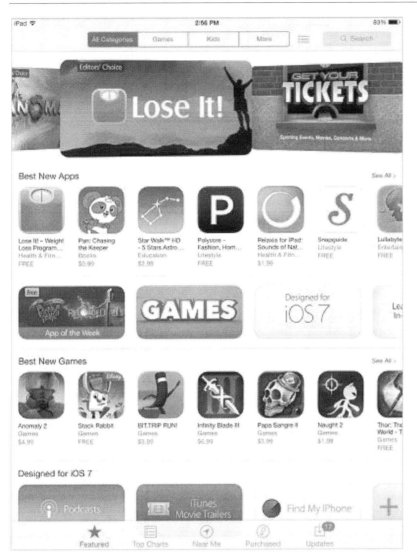

Figure 5: Application Store

Figure 6: Matching Application Store Results

Browse by Category

To browse applications by category, touch the ![icon] icon. The Application Store opens. Touch a category at the top of the screen, or touch More to view more categories, and touch a category. A list of applications in the selected category appears, as shown in **Figure 7** (applications for kids).

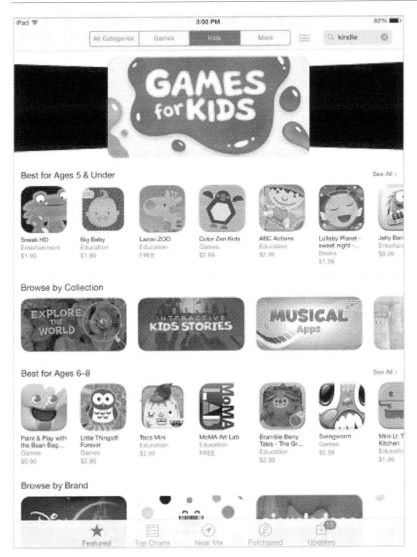

Figure 7: List of Applications in a Category (Applications for Kids)

To browse applications by popularity:

- Touch the icon. The Application Store opens.
- Touch the icon at the bottom of the screen. The Top Charts screen appears, as shown in **Figure 8** .
- Touch one of the following to browse applications:
    - **Free** - View the most popular free applications.
    - **Top Grossing** - View the most popular applications that have earned their creators the most money.

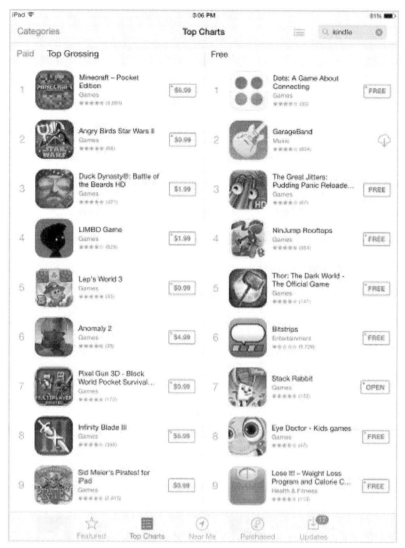

Figure 8: Top Charts Screen

5. Buying an Application

You may purchase applications directly from your iPad. To buy an application:

1. Touch the ⓐ icon. The Application Store opens.
2. Find an application. Refer to *"Searching for an Application to Purchase"* on page 138 to learn how.
3. Touch an application in the list. The Application description appears, as shown in **Figure 9**.

4. Touch the price of the application or the word **FREE** next to the name of the application. 'BUY' appears if the application is paid, or 'INSTALL' appears if the application is free. If the application is already downloaded to your iPad, 'OPEN' appears.

   Touch **BUY** or **INSTALL**. The password prompt appears.

5. Enter your iTunes password and touch **OK**. The iPad returns to the Home screen and the application is downloaded and installed.

Figure 9: Application Description

6. Using Wi-Fi to Download an Application

Applications that are over 10MB in size require the iPad to be connected to a Wi-Fi network to download. These applications will display the following message: "Application over 10MB. Connect to a Wi-Fi network or use iTunes on your computer to download >APP NAME<'", where APP NAME refers to the name of the application you are trying to download. Refer to *"Setting Up Wi-Fi"* on page 12 to learn how to turn on Wi-Fi.

7. Switching Between Applications

The iPad allows you to switch between running applications without having to exit any of them. For instance, you can listen to Pandora radio and read an eBook at the same time. To switch between applications:

1. Touch an application icon on one of your Home screens. The application opens.
2. Press the **Home** button. The Home screen is shown.
3. Open another application. Press the **Home** button twice quickly. All of the open applications are displayed, as shown in **Figure 10**.
4. Touch an application icon. The iPad switches to the selected application.

Note: When switching to another application, the first application is never automatically closed. The application is simply running in the background. Refer to "Closing an Application Running in the Background" *on page 145 to learn how to close an application.*

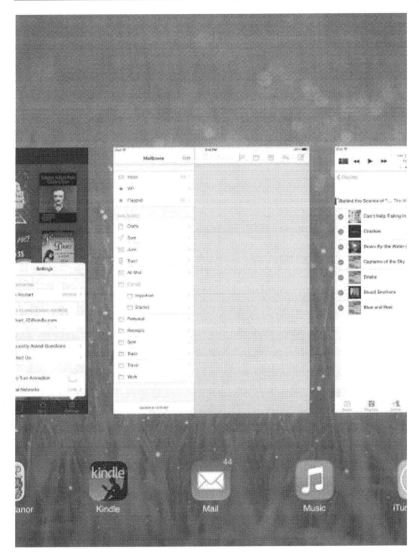

Figure 10: Open Applications

8. Closing an Application Running in the Background

After pressing the Home button to exit an application, it is not closed, but is left running in the background instead. It is good to have the application running, because you can always switch to it quickly. However, if an application stops responding or if your battery is dying too quickly, you may wish to close it. To close an application running in the background, press the **Home** button twice quickly. All of the open applications are displayed. Touch and hold an application icon and slide your finger up. The application is closed. You can also close multiple applications at the same time by touching two or more applications at the same time and sliding your fingers up. Switch to an open application by touching it in the list.

9. Organizing Applications into Folders

To create an application folder, touch and hold an application icon and drag it on top of another icon. The folder is created. To remove an application from a folder, touch and hold it, and drag it outside of the folder.

10. Reading User Reviews

In order to make a more informed decision when purchasing an application, you can read the reviews written by other users. However, be aware that people who have not used the application can also post reviews, which are uninformed. To read user reviews for an application:

1. Touch the ![App Store icon] icon. The Application Store opens.
2. Find the application that you want. Refer to *"Searching for an Application to Purchase"* on page 138 to learn how.
3. Touch an application icon. The Application description appears.
4. Touch **Reviews** below the name of the application. The reviews for the application appear.

11. Changing Application Settings

Some applications have settings that can be changed from the Settings screen. To change the Application settings, touch the ![Settings icon] icon. The Settings screen appears. Scroll down and touch an application below 'Game Center' at the bottom of the screen. The Application Settings screen appears. The settings on this screen depend on the particular application.

12. Deleting an Application

You may delete most applications from your iPad to free up space on your memory card or Home screen. To delete an unwanted application:

1. Touch and hold an application icon. All of the applications on the Home screen begin to shake. Applications that can be erased have an ![X button] button in their top left corner.

2. Touch the ![X button] button next to an application icon. A confirmation dialog appears.

3. Touch **Delete**. The application is deleted.

4. Press the **Home** button. The application icons stop shaking and the buttons disappear.

Note: If you delete a paid application, you can download it again free of charge at any time. Refer to "Buying an Application" on page 142 and follow the instructions for buying the application to re-download it.

13. Sending an Application as a Gift

On the iPad Air, applications can be sent as gifts directly to someone's email. To send an application as a gift:

1. Touch the icon. The Application Store opens.
2. Find the application that you want to give as a gift. Refer to *"Searching for an Application to Purchase"* on page 138 to learn how.
3. Touch the application icon. The application description appears.
4. Touch the icon in the upper right-hand corner of the screen. The Application options appear, as shown in **Figure 11**.
5. Touch **Gift**. The Send Gift screen appears, as shown in **Figure 12**.
6. Touch **To:** and enter the email address of the recipient of the gift. Enter an optional message.
7. Touch **Today** to select when the gift should be shared, if the date is other than the current day.
8. Touch **Next** in the upper right-hand corner of the screen. The Theme Selection screen appears.
9. Select a theme and touch **Next** in the upper right-hand corner of the screen. The Gift Confirmation screen appears, as shown in **Figure 13**.
10. Touch **Buy** in the upper right-hand corner of the screen. 'BUY NOW' appears as a confirmation.
11. Touch **BUY NOW**. The password prompt appears.
12. Enter your iTunes password and touch **OK**. The gift is purchased and sent.

Note: You are charged for the gifted application as soon as you purchase it.

Figure 11: Application Options

Figure 12: Send Gift Screen

Figure 13: Gift Confirmation Screen

14. Redeeming a Gifted Application

When receiving an application as a gift, you must redeem it in order to download it. To redeem a gift and download the application using your iPad:

1. Touch the  icon. The email application opens.
2. Touch the email with the subject **'NAME sent you an iTunes Gift'**, where NAME represents the name of the sender. The email opens. Refer to *"Reading Email"* on page 102 to learn how to find an email.

3. Touch the **Redeem Now** button in the email. The Application Store opens.

4. Touch **Redeem** in the upper right-hand corner of the screen. The gifted application is downloaded and installed. If the application is over 10MB, you must first turn on Wi-Fi. Refer to *"Setting Up Wi-Fi"* on page 12 to learn how to turn Wi-Fi on. If this is your first time downloading an application from the iTunes store, you will need to touch **Agree** several times to accept several pages of terms and conditions.

15. Turning Automatic Application Updates On or Off

The iPad can automatically download updates for applications when new versions are released. To turn automatic application updates on or off:

1. Touch the ⚙ icon. The Settings screen appears.

2. Scroll down and touch **iTunes & App Store**. The iTunes & App Store Settings screen appears.

3. Touch the ⬜ switch next to 'Updates' under 'Automatic Downloads'. The switch appears and Automatic application updates are turned off.

4. Touch the ⬤ switch next to 'Updates' under 'Automatic Downloads'. The switch appears and Automatic application updates are turned on.

Using the FaceTime Application

Table of Contents

1. Setting Up FaceTime

FaceTime is a video conferencing application, which was first introduced on the iPhone 4. The iPad Air can use its front-facing and rear-facing cameras to run this application. Before using FaceTime for the first time, you must set up the application. To set up FaceTime:

1. Make sure that Wi-Fi is turned on. Refer to *"Setting Up Wi-Fi"* on page 12 to learn how to turn on Wi-Fi.

2. Touch the ▢ icon. The FaceTime application opens and the Login screen appears, as shown in **Figure 1**.

3. Enter your Apple ID email and password and touch **Sign In**. FaceTime signs in to your account and the Address screen appears. Refer to *"Logging in to the Application Store"* on page 22 to learn how to create a new Apple ID.

4. Touch the 'Address' field to enter a different email address where callers may reach you. The alternate email address is entered.

5. Touch **Next**. FaceTime setup is complete and a list of FaceTime contacts appears if you have contacts stored in the Address Book, as shown in **Figure 2**.

Note: You may collectively manage FaceTime and email contacts using the Address book. Refer to "Managing Contacts" *on page 122 to learn how.*

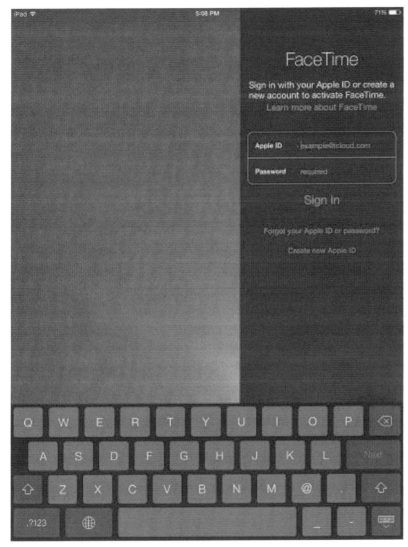

Figure 1: FaceTime Login Screen

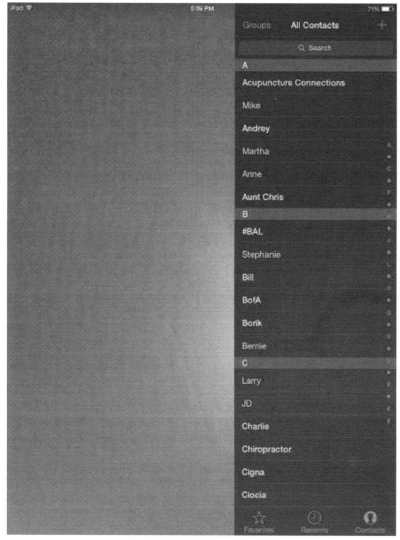

Figure 2: FaceTime Contacts

2. Placing a FaceTime Call

Using the FaceTime application, the iPad Air can place a video call to another iPad (second or third generation), iPhone 4 or later, or Mac. To place a FaceTime call:

1. Touch the ▣ icon. The FaceTime application opens and a list of your contacts appears.
2. Touch a contact's name. The contact's information appears.
3. Touch a phone number or email. The iPad places a FaceTime call. The contact receives a FaceTime call, as shown in **Figure 3** (iPod Touch). Calling a device that is not compatible with FaceTime will result in an error, as shown in **Figure 4**.

4. Touch the button (on recipient's side). A FaceTime call begins, as shown in **Figure 5**.

5. Touch the button at any time to switch cameras. The rear-facing camera is selected.

6. Touch **End** at any time to end the call. The call ends.

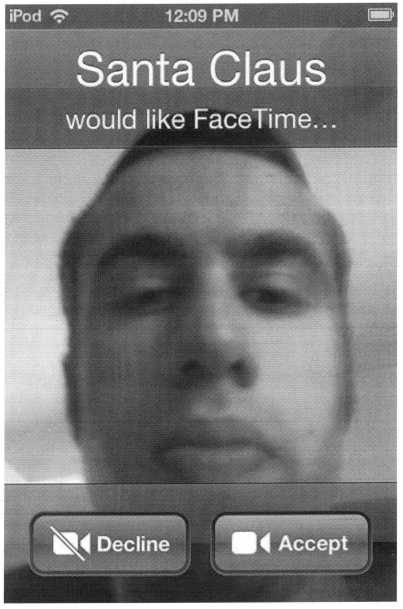

Figure 3: Receiving a FaceTime Call on an iPod Touch

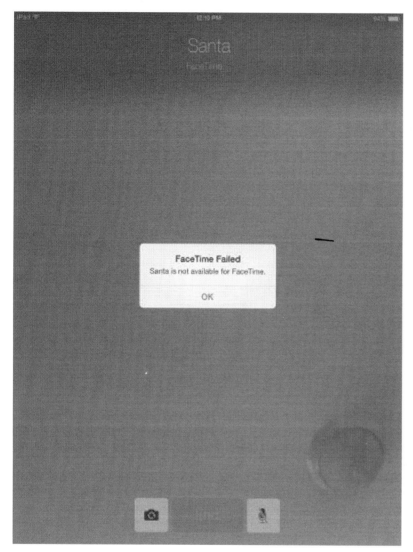

Figure 4: FaceTime Call Error

Figure 5: Active FaceTime Call

3. Receiving a FaceTime Call

Using the FaceTime application, the iPad Air can receive a video call from another iPad (second or third generation), iPhone 4 or later, Mac, or iPod Touch. If your iPad is locked when you receive a FaceTime call, the Locked Incoming FaceTime Call screen appears, as shown in **Figure 6**. If your iPad is unlocked when you receive a FaceTime call, the Unlocked Incoming FaceTime Call screen appears, as shown in **Figure 7**. To receive a FaceTime call:

1. Touch the ⟩ slide to answer bar and slide your finger to the right if your iPad is locked. Touch **Answer** if your iPad is unlocked. The FaceTime call begins.

2. Touch the 📷 button at any time to switch cameras. The rear-facing camera turns on.

3. Touch the 📷 button again. The front-facing camera turns on.

4. Touch **End** at any time to end the FaceTime call. The call ends.

Figure 6: Incoming FaceTime Call, iPad Locked

Figure 7: Incoming FaceTime Call, iPad Unlocked

4. Moving the Picture-in-Picture Display

The Picture-in-Picture display shows you what the FaceTime caller is currently seeing by showing your mug shot in a small box on the screen. By default, the Picture-in-Picture display is located in the bottom right corner of the screen. To move your mug shot, touch and hold the frame and drag it to another corner.

Note: The Picture-in-Picture display cannot be moved to a location other than one of the four corners of the screen.

5. Muting the Microphone

The microphone may be muted during a FaceTime call to prevent the caller from hearing your side

of the conversation. Touch the  button at any time to mute the microphone.

Note: The caller will still be able to see you while the microphone is muted.

Using the iBooks Application

Table of Contents

1. Installing iBooks

Before you can read eBooks from the iBooks store, you must download the iBooks application. To download and install iBooks:

1. Search for the iBooks application in the Application store. Refer to *"Searching for an Application to Purchase"* on page 138 to learn how.
2. Touch **iBooks** in the matching search results. The iBooks description appears, as shown in **Figure 1**.
3. Touch **FREE**. 'INSTALL' appears.
4. Touch **INSTALL**. The Password prompt appears.
5. Enter your iTunes password and touch **OK**. iBooks is downloaded and installed.

Figure 1: iBooks Description

2. Finding an eBook to Purchase

You may search for eBooks directly from the iBooks application. To search for eBooks:

- Touch the ⬚ icon on the Home screen. The iBooks application opens, as shown in **Figure 2**. If you have purchased eBooks in iBooks in the past, the Sync dialog appears. Touch **Sync** to import your eBooks into iBooks, or touch **Don't Sync** to prevent iBooks from syncing.

- Touch the **Store** button in the upper left-hand corner of the screen. The iBooks Store opens, as shown in **Figure 3**.

- Use one of the following methods to find an eBook:

    - Touch **Search** at the top of the screen and enter the name of an eBook or author.
    - Touch **Top Authors** at the bottom of the screen to view the bestselling authors.
    - Touch **Top Charts** at the bottom of the screen to view the top selling and top free eBooks.
    - Touch **Purchased** at the bottom of the screen to view downloaded eBooks.

Figure 2: iBooks Application

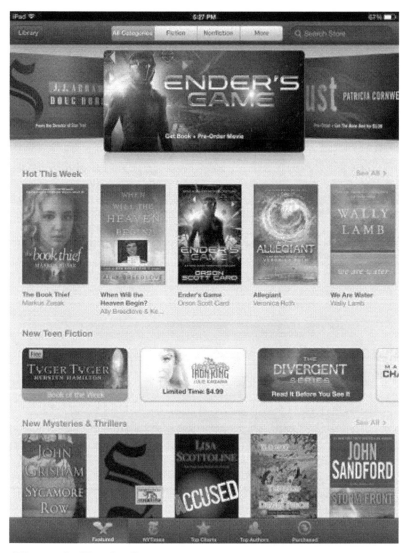

Figure 3: iBooks Store

3. Buying an eBook

You may buy eBooks directly from the iBooks application. To buy an eBook:

1. Touch the 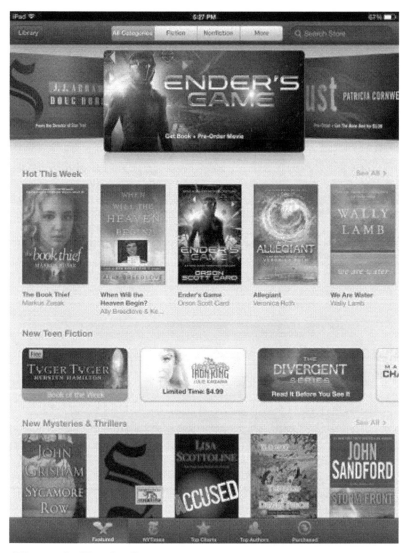 icon. The iBooks application opens.
2. Touch the **Store** button at the top right of the screen. The iBooks Store opens.
3. Find the eBook that you wish to buy. Refer to *"Finding an eBook to Purchase"* on page 162 to learn how.
4. Touch the price of the eBook. 'BUY BOOK' appears in its place.

5. Touch **BUY BOOK** if the eBook is paid, or touch **FREE** and then **GET BOOK** if the eBook is free. The password prompt appears.

6. Enter your iTunes password and touch **OK**. The eBook is downloaded and appears on the iBooks bookshelf.

4. Downloading Previously Purchased eBooks (iBooks Application)

After purchasing an eBook on another Apple device, you may download it to your iPad at any time for free. To download a previously purchased eBook:

1. Touch the [icon] icon. The iBooks application opens.

2. Touch the [Store] in the upper right-hand corner of the screen. The iBooks store opens.

3. Touch **Purchased** in the lower right-hand corner of the screen. The Purchased screen appears, as shown in **Figure 4**.

4. Touch the [button] button next to the eBook that you wish to download. The eBook is downloaded to your iBooks library. If the password prompt appears, enter your password and touch **OK**.

Note: If you do not see the eBook that you wish to download, try touching **Not On This iPad** *at the top of the screen to browse your other purchased eBooks.*

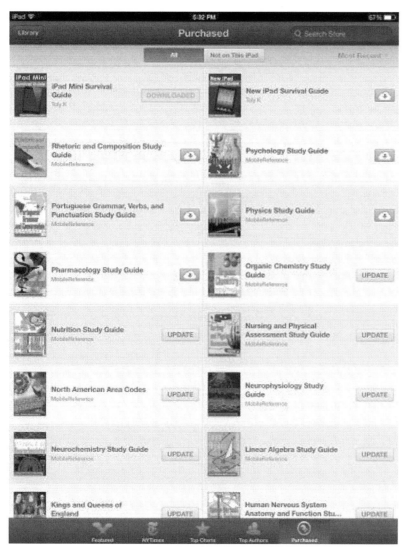

Figure 4: Purchased Screen

5. Turning On Automatic eBook Downloads

You can set your iPad to automatically download any eBooks purchased on other Apple devices. To turn on Automatic eBook Downloads:

1. Touch the ⚙ icon. The Settings screen appears.

2. Scroll down and touch **iTunes & App Store**. If you are signed in, the Store Settings screen appears, as shown in **Figure 5**. Otherwise, touch **Apple ID** and enter your Apple credentials.

3. Touch the ⬭ switch next to 'Books' on the Store Settings screen. The ⬬ switch appears, and Automatic eBook Downloads are turned on. You can always touch the ⬬ switch next to 'Books' to turn off the feature.

Figure 5: iTunes & App Store Settings Screen

6. Reading an eBook

You can read eBooks on your iPad. While reading, use the following tips to navigate an eBook:

- **Turning Pages** - Move your finger across the screen to the left or right to flip the pages. You can also touch the left or right edge of the screen to turn the page.

- **Skipping to a Page** - Touch the center of the page and then drag the cursor at the bottom of the page along the dotted line to skip to a desired page. (The cursor will not appear until the eBook is fully loaded.)

- **Adding a Bookmark** - Touch the center of the page and then touch the icon in the upper right-hand corner. A icon appears in the upper right-hand corner of the page to signify a bookmark.

- **Defining a Word -** Touch a word twice in succession. The Word menu appears. Touch **Define**. The word definition appears.

- **Viewing in Landscape Mode** - Rotate the iPad to switch between Landscape and Portrait mode.

- **Zooming In on an Image -** Touch an image twice in rapid succession. The image appears in full-screen view.

7. Highlighting Text and Taking Notes

While reading an eBook, you may highlight passages and take notes for future reference. To highlight a passage:

1. Touch and hold a word. The highlight markers and the Text menu appear, as shown in **Figure 6**.
2. Touch the markers and drag them to select text. The text is selected
3. Touch **Highlight**. The text is highlighted, as shown in **Figure 7**.

To take notes in an eBook:

1. Touch and hold a word. The highlight markers and the Text menu appear.
2. Touch **Note**. A post-it note appears, as shown in **Figure 8**.
3. Enter a note. Touch **Done** in the upper right-hand corner of the screen. The note is added and the icon appears in the page margin.

4. Touch the icon at any time. The note appears.

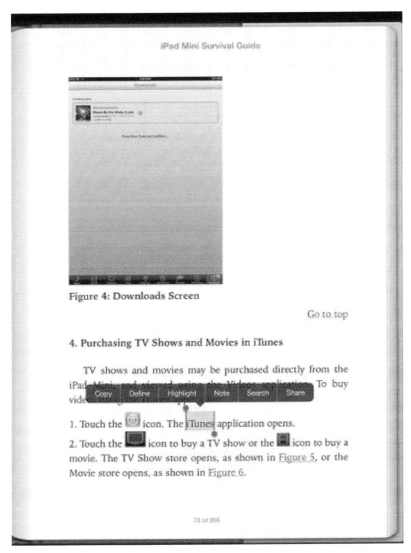

Figure 6: Highlight Markers and Text Menu

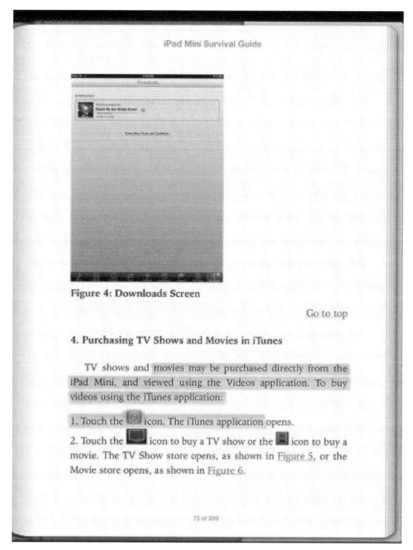

Figure 7: Highlighted Text

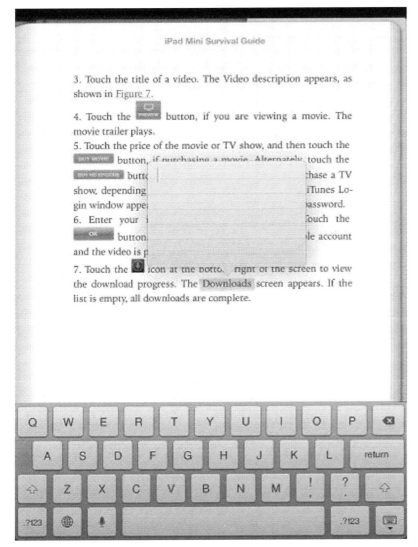

Figure 8: Post-It Note

8. Changing the Font and Text Size

To change the font and text size while reading:

1. Touch the center of the page. The eBook menu appears at the top of the screen, as shown in **Figure 9**.
2. Touch the AA icon at the top of the screen. The Font menu appears, as shown in **Figure 10**.
3. Touch the larger 'A' to increase the font size, or touch the smaller 'A' to decrease it. The font size is adjusted accordingly.
4. Touch **Fonts**. A list of available fonts appears.

5. Touch a font name. The font is changed accordingly.
6. Touch anywhere outside of the eBook menu. The eBook menu is closed.

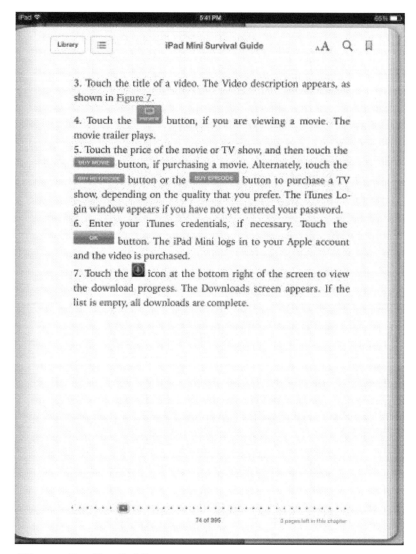

Figure 9: eBook Menu

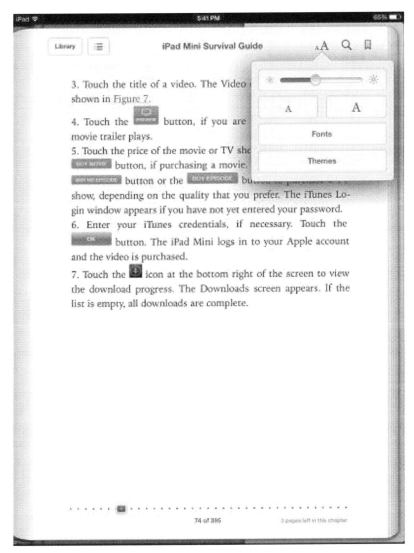

Figure 10: Font Menu

9. Searching an eBook

You may search an eBook for a specific word or phrase. To search an eBook while reading:

1. Touch the Q icon at the top of the screen. The Search field appears.
2. Enter a word or phrase and touch **Search**. The matching search results appear below the field.
3. Touch a search result to navigate to the page where it is located. The word or phrase is highlighted on the page, as shown in **Figure 11**.

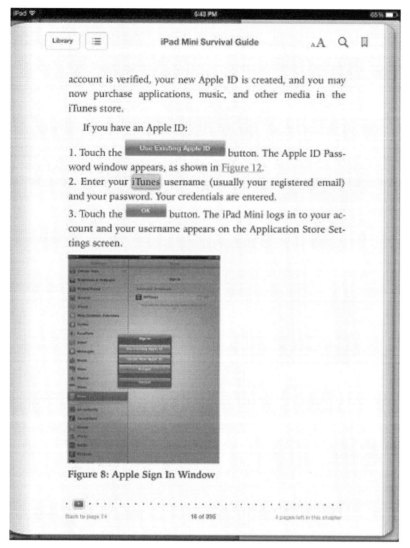

Figure 11: Highlighted Search Result

10. Sorting and Deleting eBooks

iBooks allows you to rearrange eBooks on your shelves or to view them in list form. iBooks also allows eBooks to be deleted. Touch **Edit** in the upper left-hand corner of the screen in the iBooks application and use the following tips to manage your eBooks:

1. Touch and hold an eBook and drag it around to move it to another location.

2. Touch an eBook and then touch the **Delete** button in the upper right-hand corner of the screen to delete it.

3. Touch the ▤ icon to view the eBooks as a list (without touching 'Edit' first).
4. Touch the ⊞ icon to view the eBooks as thumbnails on bookshelves (without touching 'Edit' first).

11. Creating and Adding eBooks to Collections

One of the newest features in iBooks is the ability to create a collection of eBooks, analogous to bookshelves. Collections are useful for organizational purposes.

To create a collection:

- In the iBooks application, touch **Collections** at the top of the screen. The Collection menu appears, as shown in **Figure 12**.
- Touch **New**. An empty field appears in the list of collections.
- Enter a name for the collection and touch **Done**. The new collection is created.
- Touch **Done** in the upper right-hand corner of the screen to return to the library.

To add eBooks to a collection:

1. In the iBooks application, touch **Edit** in the upper right-hand corner of the screen. The Editing menu appears.

2. Touch as many eBooks as desired. The ✓ icons appear on the selected eBooks.

3. Touch the Move button in the upper left-hand corner of the screen. A list of collections appears.

4. Touch the name of a collection. The eBooks are added to the selected collection, and the collection opens.

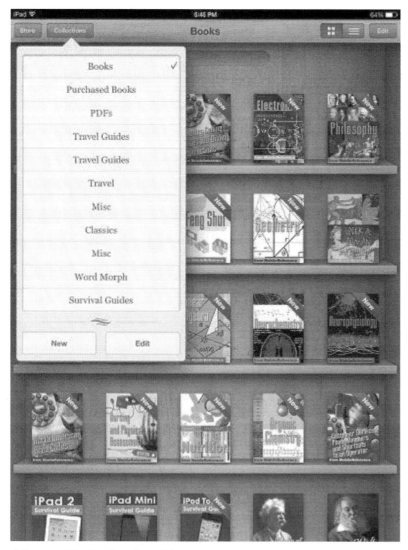

Figure 12: Collection Menu

12. Updating an eBook to a Newer Version

To update an eBook in iBooks, first delete the eBook and then re-download it. To update an eBook to a newer version:

1. Delete the eBook from the library. Refer to *"Sorting and Deleting eBooks"* on page 174 to learn how.

2. Touch the **Store** button in the upper right-hand corner of the screen. The iBooks Store opens.

3. Touch **Purchases** in the bottom right-hand corner of the screen. All previous purchases are shown.

4. Find the eBook that you just deleted and touch the button. The password prompt appears.

5. Enter your iTunes password and touch **OK**. The updated eBook is downloaded and appears in the iBooks library.

13. Sending Suggestions and Reporting Bugs

If you find any software bugs or have suggestions for improving Apple's iBooks application, you may contact the iBooks development team directly at **ibookstore@apple.com**.

Using Siri

Table of Contents

1. Making a Call

To make a call using Siri, press and hold the **Home** button and wait for Siri to speak. Say one of the following phrases:

- **FaceTime John** (use any name)
- **FaceTime Suzy on her Mobile**

Note: These phrases are only suggestions. Siri is flexible, and you can use many synonymous phrases.

2. Sending and Receiving Text Messages

To send, read, or reply to a text message using Siri, press and hold the **Home** button and wait for Siri to speak. Say one of the following phrases:

- **Tell Anne See you soon**
- **Send a message to Rob Burr**
- **Send a message to Larry saying What's your address?**
- **Send a message to Julie on her mobile saying I got an iPad Air!**

- **Send a message to 999 555 2222**
- **Text Jude and Prudence What are you guys up to today?**
- **Read my new messages**
- **Read it again**
- **Reply that's great news**
- **Tell him ETA is 20 minutes**
- **Call her**

Note: These phrases are only suggestions. Siri is flexible, and you can use many synonymous phrases.

3. Managing the Address Book

To manage the address book using Siri, press and hold the **Home** button and wait for Siri to speak. Say one of the following phrases:

- **What's Joe's address?**
- **What is Susan Park's phone number?**
- **When is my grandfather's birthday?**
- **Show Bobby's email address**
- **Show Pete Abred**
- **Find people named Apple**
- **My brother is Trudy Ages** (assigns a relationship to the name)
- **Who is Colin Card?** (indicates Colin Card's relationship to you)
- **Call my brother at home** (calls the number assigned to the relationship)

Note: These phrases are only suggestions. Siri is flexible, and you can use many synonymous phrases.

4. Setting Up and Managing Meetings

To set up and manage meetings using Siri, press and hold the **Home** button and wait for Siri to speak. Say one of the following phrases:
- **Set up a meeting at 10**
- **Set up a meeting with Zoe at 9**
- **Meet with Nikki at noon**
- **New appointment with Dan Delion Tuesday at 4**
- **Schedule a focus group meeting at 3:30 today in the boardroom**

- **Move my 2pm meeting to 3:30**
- **Add Wendy to my meeting with Waldo**
- **Cancel the focus group meeting**
- **What does the rest of my day look like?**
- **What's on my calendar for Monday?**
- **When is my next appointment?**
- **Where is my next meeting?**

Note: These phrases are only suggestions. Siri is flexible, and you can use many synonymous phrases.

5. Checking the Time and Setting Alarms

To check the time and set alarms using Siri, press and hold the **Home** button and wait for Siri to speak. Say one of the following phrases:

- **Wake me up tomorrow at 6am**
- **Set an alarm for 6:30am**
- **Wake me up in 8 hours**
- **Change my 5:30 alarm to 6:30**
- **Turn off my 4:30 alarm**
- **What time is it?**
- **What time is it in Moscow?**
- **What is today's date?**
- **What's the date this Friday?**
- **Set the timer for 30 minutes**
- **Show the timer**
- **Pause the timer**
- **Resume**
- **Reset the timer**
- **Stop it**

Note: These phrases are only suggestions. Siri is flexible, and you can use many synonymous phrases.

6. Sending and Receiving Email

To send and receive email using Siri, press and hold the **Home** button and wait for Siri to speak. Say one of the following phrases:

- **Email Dave about the trip**
- **Email New email to John Diss**
- **Mail Dad about dinner**
- **Email Dr. Spaulding and say Got your message**
- **Mail Jack and Jill about the party and say It was awesome**
- **Check email**
- **Any new email from Mom today?**
- **Show new mail about the apartment**
- **Show the email from Roger yesterday**
- **Reply Dear Mark I'm sorry for your loss**

Note: These phrases are only suggestions. Siri is flexible, and you can use many synonymous phrases.

7. Getting Directions and Finding Businesses

To get directions and find businesses using Siri, press and hold the **Home** button and wait for Siri to speak. Say one of the following phrases:

- **How do I get home?**
- **Show 10 Park Ave. Boston Massachusetts**
- **Directions to my parents' home**
- **Find coffee near meWhere is Starbucks?**
- **Find a Mexican restaurant in New Mexico**
- **Find a gas station within walking distance**

Note: These phrases are only suggestions. Siri is flexible, and you can use many synonymous phrases.

8. Playing Music

To play music using Siri, press and hold the **Home** button and wait for Siri to speak. Say one of the following phrases:

- **Play Hotel California**
- **Play Coldplay shuffled**
- **Play Dave Matthews Band**
- **Play some folk**
- **Play my roadtrip playlist**
- **Shuffle my party playlist**
- **Play**
- **Pause**
- **Skip**

Note: These phrases are only suggestions. Siri is flexible, and you can use many synonymous phrases.

9. Searching the Web and Asking Questions

To search the web using Siri, press and hold the **Home** button and wait for Siri to speak. Say one of the following phrases:

- **Search the web for Apple News**
- **Search for chili recipes**
- **Google the humane society**
- **Search Wikipedia for Duckbilled Platypus**
- **Bing Secondhand Serenade**
- **How many calories in a doughnut?**
- **What is an 18% tip on $180.45 for six people?**
- **How long do cats live?**
- **What's 25 squared?**
- **How many dollars is 60 euros?**
- **How many days until Christmas?**
- **When is the next solar eclipse?**
- **Show me the Ursula Major constellation**
- **What is the meaning of life?**
- **What's the price of gasoline in Boston?**

Note: These phrases are only suggestions. Siri is flexible, and you can use many synonymous phrases.

10. Looking Up Words in the Dictionary

To look up words using Siri, press and hold the **Home** button and wait for Siri to speak. Say one of the following phrases:

- **What is the meaning of meticulous?**
- **Define albeit**
- **Look up the word jargon**

Note: These phrases are only suggestions. Siri is flexible, and you can use many phrases synonymous with these suggestions.

Adjusting Wireless Settings

Table of Contents

1. Turning Airplane Mode On or Off

Most airplanes do not allow wireless communications while in flight. Continue using the iPad by enabling Airplane mode before take-off. You may not place or receive calls, send or receive text messages or emails, or surf the Web while in Airplane mode. Airplane Mode is also useful when traveling outside of your area of service to avoid any roaming charges and to preserve battery life. To turn Airplane Mode on or off:

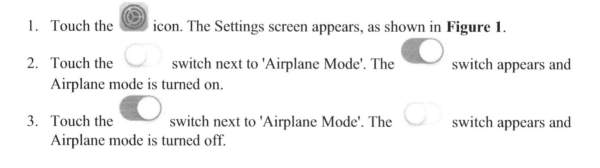

1. Touch the icon. The Settings screen appears, as shown in **Figure 1**.

2. Touch the switch next to 'Airplane Mode'. The switch appears and Airplane mode is turned on.

3. Touch the switch next to 'Airplane Mode'. The switch appears and Airplane mode is turned off.

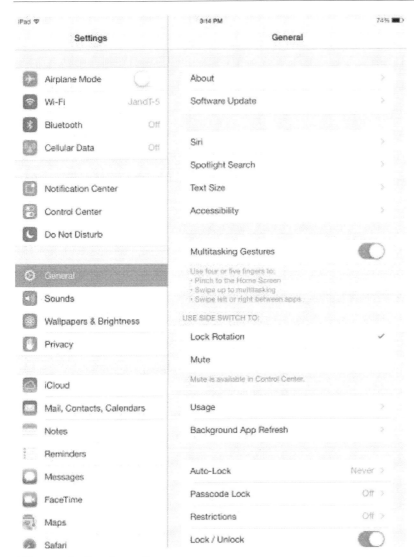

Figure 1: Settings Screen

2. Turning Location Services On or Off

Some iPad applications require the Location Services feature to be turned on, which determines your current location. To turn Location Services on or off:

1. Touch the ⊚ icon. The Settings screen appears.
2. Scroll down and touch **Privacy**. The Privacy Settings screen appears, as shown in **Figure 2**.
3. Touch **Location Services**. The Location Services screen appears, as shown in **Figure 3**.

4. Touch the ⬤ switch next to 'Location Services'. The ⬤ switch appears and Location Services are turned on.

5. Touch the ⬤ switch next to 'Location Services'. The ⬤ switch appears and Location Services are turned off.

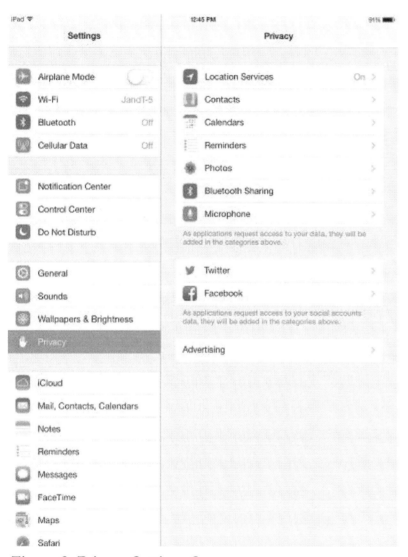

Figure 2: Privacy Settings Screen

Figure 3: Location Services Screen

3. Turning 4G On or Off (4G Models Only)

Using the 4G network will allow data to be accessed faster than on 2G. Surfing the internet and downloading applications is also faster. However, you can turn 4G off if you wish to conserve battery life. To turn 4G on or off:

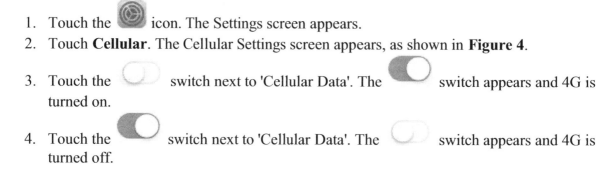

1. Touch the ⊚ icon. The Settings screen appears.
2. Touch **Cellular**. The Cellular Settings screen appears, as shown in **Figure 4**.

3. Touch the ⬭ switch next to 'Cellular Data'. The ⬭ switch appears and 4G is turned on.

4. Touch the ⬭ switch next to 'Cellular Data'. The ⬭ switch appears and 4G is turned off.

Note: Turning 4G on in an area where AT&T or Verizon has no 4G coverage will result in the iPad's having no access to the wireless network. This will result in the iPad's battery dying more quickly, as it will continue to search for service. In this case, simply turn 4G off to regain normal 2G coverage.

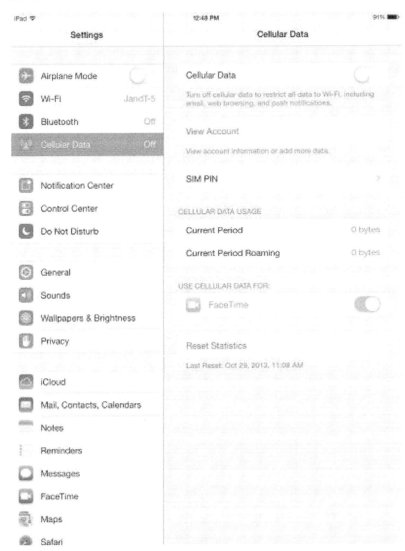

Figure 4: Cellular Settings Screen

4. Turning Data Roaming On or Off

When you are in an area with no wireless coverage, the iPad can use the Data Roaming feature to acquire signal from other networks. Be aware that Data Roaming can be extremely costly. Contact your network provider for details. You cannot turn on Data Roaming if Cellular Data is turned off. To turn Data Roaming on or off:

1. Touch the ![icon] icon. The Settings screen appears.
2. Touch **Cellular**. The Cellular Settings screen appears. Make sure that Cellular Data is turned on.

3. Touch the ⬭ switch next to 'Data Roaming'. The 🔘 switch appears and Data Roaming is turned on.

4. Touch the 🔘 switch next to 'Data Roaming'. The ⬭ switch appears and Data Roaming is turned off.

5. Setting Up a Virtual Private Network (VPN)

You can use your iPad to connect to an external network, such as a corporate one. To set up a VPN:

1. Touch the ⬭ icon. The Settings screen appears.
2. Touch **General**. The General Settings screen appears, as shown in **Figure 5**.
3. Touch **VPN**. The VPN screen appears, as shown in **Figure 6**.
4. Touch the ⬭ switch next to 'VPN'. The Add Configuration screen appears, as shown in **Figure 7**.
5. Touch each field and enter the required information. Touch **Save** in the upper right-hand corner of the screen when you are finished. The VPN is set up.

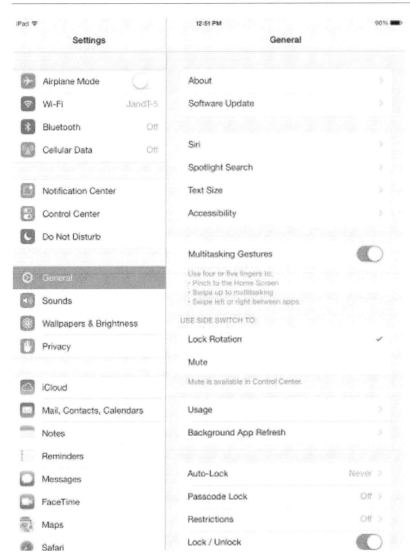

Figure 5: General Settings Screen

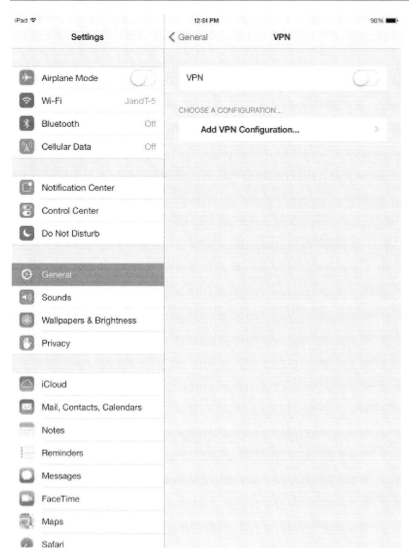

Figure 6: VPN Screen

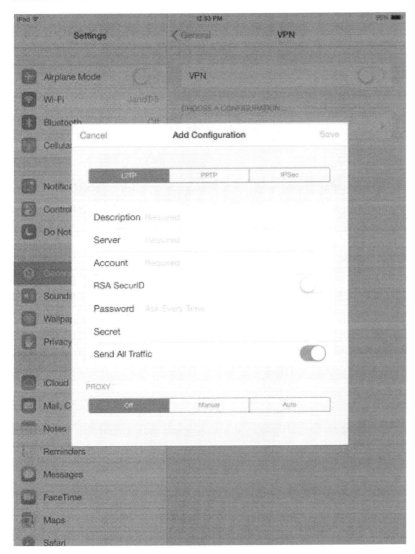

Figure 7: Add Configuration Screen

6. Turning Bluetooth On or Off

A wireless Bluetooth headset or keyboard can be used with the iPad. Be aware that leaving Bluetooth turned on while the headset is not in use may drain your battery more quickly than usual. To turn Bluetooth on or off:

1. Touch the ⚙ icon. The Settings screen appears.
2. Touch **General**. The General Settings screen appears.
3. Touch **Bluetooth**. The Bluetooth Settings screen appears, as shown in **Figure 8**.

4. Touch the ⬭ switch next to 'Bluetooth'. Bluetooth is turned on and a list of devices appears, as shown in **Figure 9**. If there are no Bluetooth devices near the iPad, the list will be empty.

5. Touch a device in the list. The iPad connects to the device.

6. Touch the ⬭ switch next to 'Bluetooth'. Bluetooth is turned off.

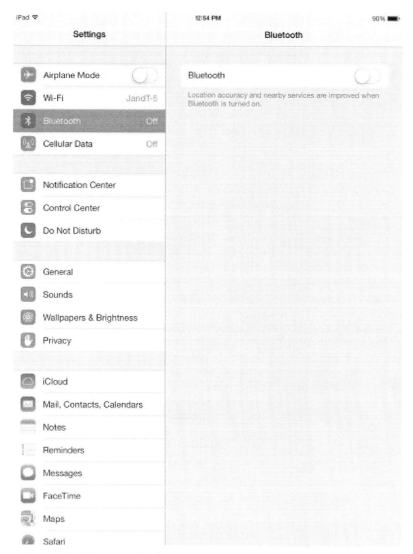

Figure 8: Bluetooth Settings Screen

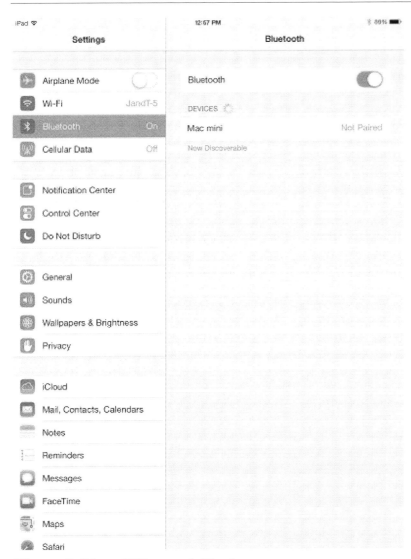

Figure 9: List of Bluetooth Devices

Adjusting Sound Settings

Table of Contents

1. Turning Volume Button Functionality On or Off

The volume buttons can be used to adjust the volume of the media, alerts, and the ringer. When the volume button functionality is disabled, they no longer work. To turn the volume button functionality on or off:

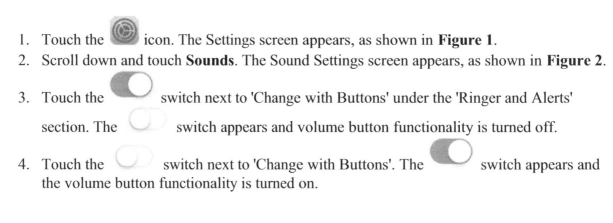

1. Touch the ⚙ icon. The Settings screen appears, as shown in **Figure 1**.
2. Scroll down and touch **Sounds**. The Sound Settings screen appears, as shown in **Figure 2**.
3. Touch the ⬤ switch next to 'Change with Buttons' under the 'Ringer and Alerts' section. The ⬤ switch appears and volume button functionality is turned off.
4. Touch the ⬤ switch next to 'Change with Buttons'. The ⬤ switch appears and the volume button functionality is turned on.

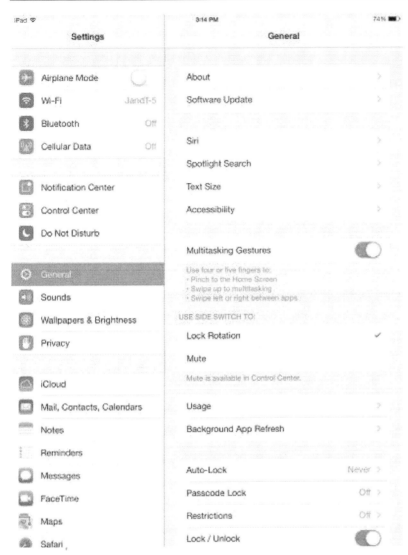

Figure 1: Settings Screen

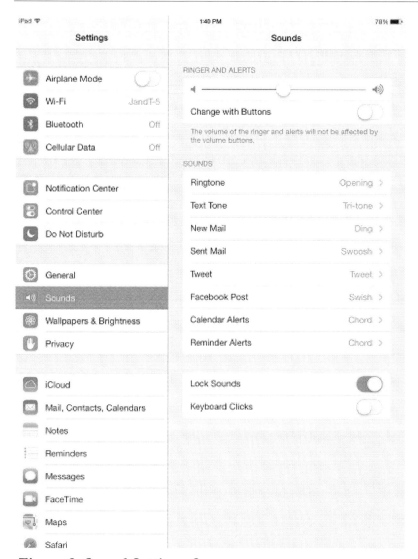

Figure 2: Sound Settings Screen

2. Setting the Default Ringtone

You may change the ringtone that sounds every time somebody calls you. To set a default ringtone:

1. Touch the 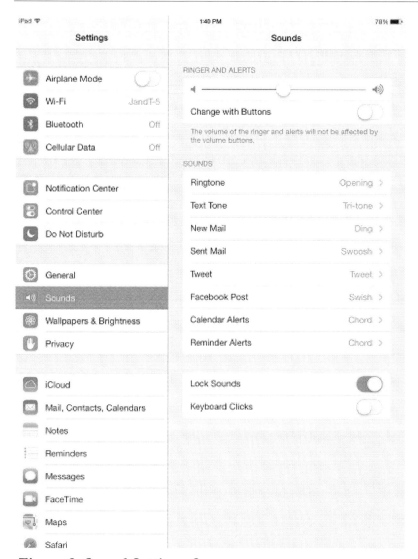 icon. The Settings screen appears.
2. Touch **Sounds**. The Sound Settings screen appears.
3. Touch **Ringtone** under the 'Sounds and Vibration Patterns' section. A list of ringtones appears, as shown in **Figure 3**.
4. Touch a ringtone. The new default ringtone is selected and a preview plays.

5. Touch **Sounds** in the upper left-hand corner of the Sound Settings screen. The new ringtone is set as the default.

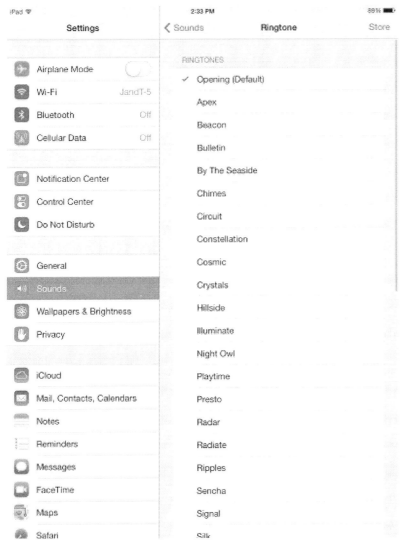

Figure 3: List of Ringtones

3. Customizing Notification and Alert Sounds

There are several notification and alert sounds that can be changed on the iPad. To customize notification and alert sounds:

1. Touch the ⚙ icon. The Settings screen appears.
2. Touch **Sounds**. The Sound Settings screen appears.
3. Touch one of the following options under the 'Sounds and Vibration Patterns' section to change the corresponding sound:

   - **Text Tone** - Plays when a new text message arrives.
   - **New Mail** - Plays when a new email arrives.
   - **Sent Mail** - Plays when an email is sent from the iPad.
   - **Tweet** - Plays when a new Tweet arrives.
   - **Facebook Post** - Plays when one of your Facebook friends creates a new post.
   - **Calendar Alerts** - Plays as a reminder for a calendar event.
   - **Reminder Alerts** - Plays as a notification of a previously set reminder.

4. Turning Lock Sounds On or Off

The iPad can make a sound every time it is locked or unlocked. By default, this sound is turned on. To turn Lock Sounds on or off:

1. Touch the ⚙ icon. The Settings screen appears
2. Touch **Sounds**. The Sound Settings screen appears.

3. Scroll down and touch the ⬤ switch next to 'Lock Sounds'. The ◯ switch appears and lock sounds are turned off.

4. Touch the ◯ switch next to 'Lock Sounds'. The ⬤ switch appears and lock sounds are turned on.

5. Turning Keyboard Clicks On or Off

The iPad can make a sound every time a key is touched on the virtual keyboard. By default, keyboard clicks are turned on. To turn Keyboard Clicks on or off:

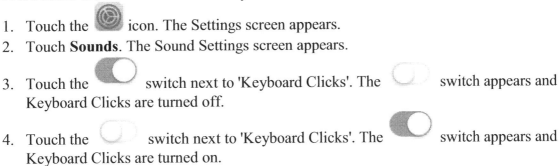

1. Touch the icon. The Settings screen appears.
2. Touch **Sounds**. The Sound Settings screen appears.
3. Touch the switch next to 'Keyboard Clicks'. The switch appears and Keyboard Clicks are turned off.
4. Touch the switch next to 'Keyboard Clicks'. The switch appears and Keyboard Clicks are turned on.

Adjusting Language and Keyboard Settings

Table of Contents

1. Customizing Spelling and Grammar Settings

Customize the Spelling and Grammar settings on your iPad to improve typing accuracy when composing text messages or emails. To customize the Spelling and Grammar settings:

1. Touch the ![settings icon] icon. The Settings screen appears, as shown in **Figure 1**.
2. Touch **General**. The General Settings screen appears, as shown in **Figure 2**.
3. Scroll down and touch **Keyboard**. The Keyboard Settings screen appears, as shown in **Figure 3**.
4. Touch one of the following switches on the right side of the screen to turn the corresponding setting on or off:

   - **Auto-Capitalization** - Capitalizes the first word of every sentence automatically.
   - **Auto-Correction** - Suggests and makes text corrections while you type.
   - **Check Spelling** - Underlines all misspelled words.

   - **Enable Caps Lock** - Allows you to turn Caps Lock on by quickly touching the ⇧ key twice on the virtual keyboard. While Caps Lock is turned on, all capital letters are typed without the need to use the ⇧ key.
   - **."" Shortcut** - Allows a period and an extra space to be inserted when you quickly touch the space bar twice.

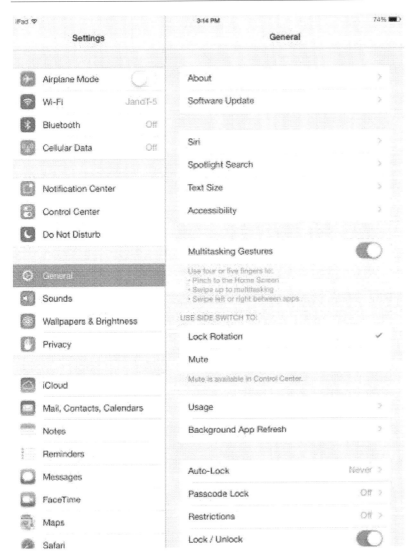

Figure 1: Settings Screen

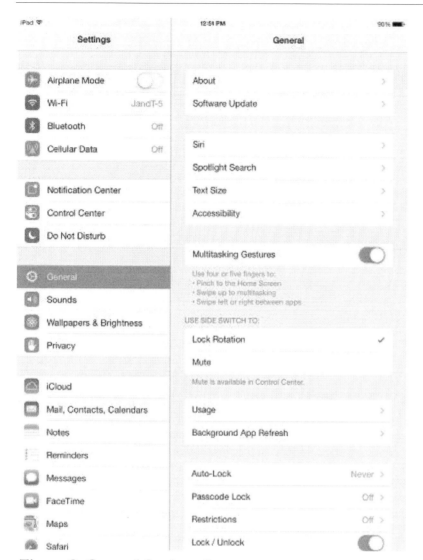

Figure 2: General Settings Screen

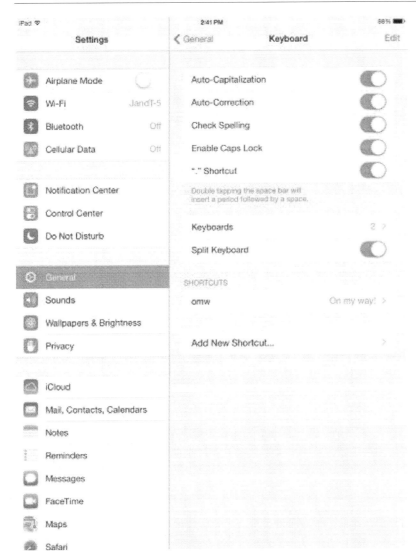

Figure 3: Keyboard Settings Screen

2. Adding an International Keyboard

The iPad allows you to use international keyboards when entering text on the virtual keyboard. To add an international keyboard:

1. Touch the 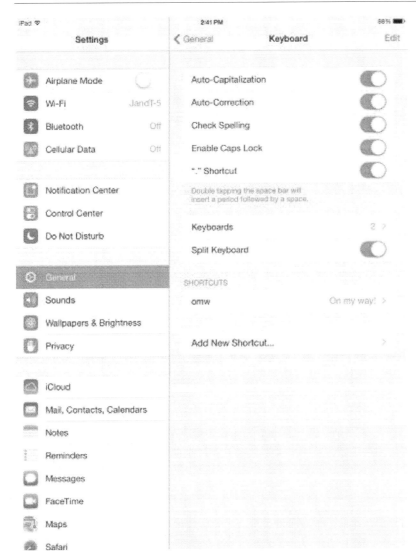 icon. The Settings screen appears.
2. Touch **General**. The General Settings screen appears.
3. Scroll down and touch **Keyboard**. The Keyboard Settings screen appears.
4. Touch **Keyboards**. The Keyboards screen appears, as shown in **Figure 4**.

5. Touch **Add New Keyboard**. A list of international keyboards appears, as shown in **Figure 5**.

6. Touch a keyboard. The keyboard is added. While typing, touch the 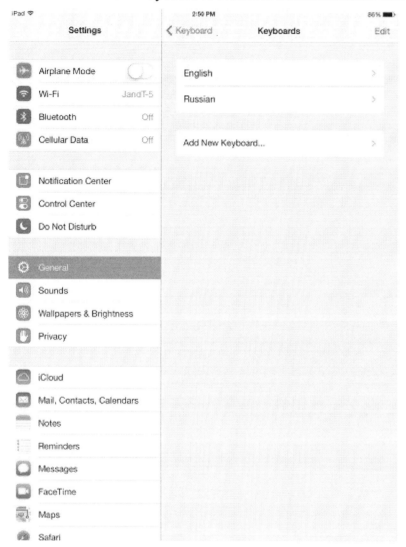 key at the bottom of the virtual keyboard to switch to an international one.

Figure 4: Keyboards Screen

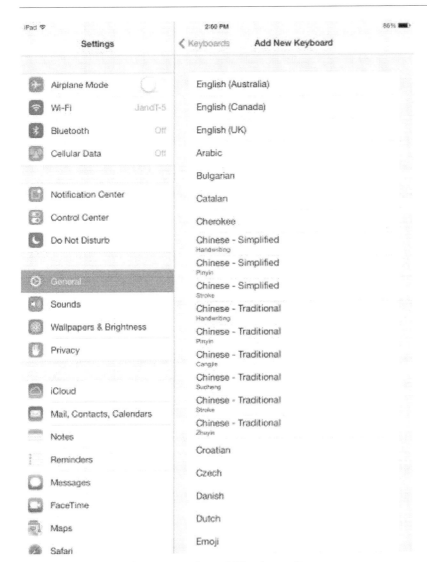

Figure 5: List of International Keyboards

3. Adding a Keyboard Shortcut

The iPad allows you to add custom Keyboard shortcuts. For example, "ur" for "your" or "ttyl" for "talk to you later" are substituted when the corresponding abbreviation is typed. To add a Keyboard shortcut:

1. Touch the 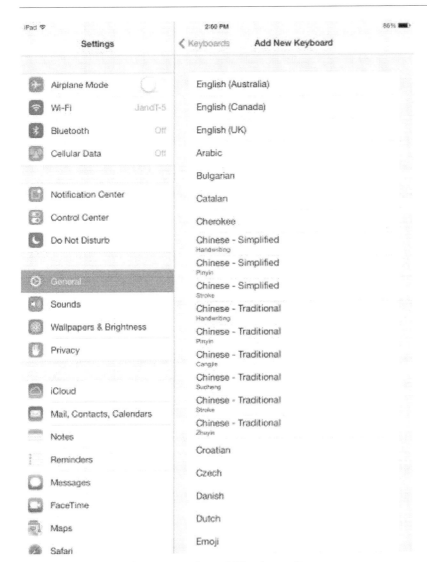 icon. The Settings screen appears.
2. Touch **General**. The General Settings screen appears.
3. Scroll down and touch **Keyboard**. The Keyboard Settings screen appears.

4. Touch **Add New Shortcut** under the 'Shortcuts' section. The Shortcut screen appears, as shown in **Figure 6**.

5. Enter the desired phrase to be substituted for the shortcut. Touch **return**.

6. Enter the desired shortcut and touch **Save** in the upper right-hand corner of the screen. The keyboard shortcut is added. To use the shortcut, type it and touch the space bar.

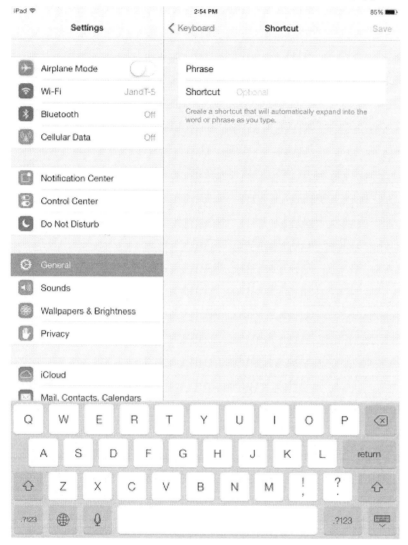

Figure 6: Shortcut Screen

4. Changing the Operating System Language

The iOS on the iPad can be changed to display all menus and options in a language other than English. To change the Operating System Language:

1. Touch the ⊚ icon. The Settings screen appears.
2. Touch **General**. The General Settings screen appears.
3. Scroll down and touch **International**. The International screen appears, as shown in **Figure 7**.
4. Touch **Language**. A list of available languages appears, as shown in **Figure 8**.
5. Touch a language and touch **Done** in the upper right-hand corner of the screen. The selected language is applied and all menus and options reflect the change.

Note: It may take some time to install the language. This delay is normal.

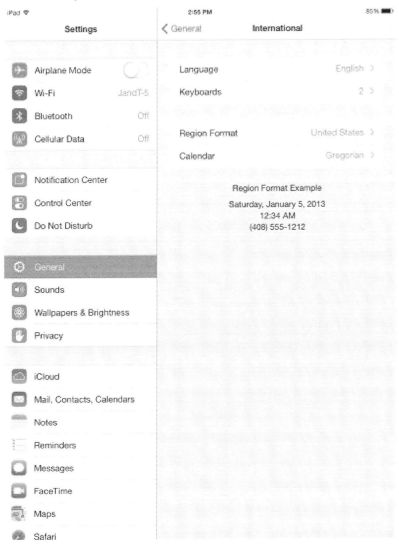

Figure 7: International Screen

Figure 8: List of Available Languages

5. Changing the Siri Language

You can change the input language that Siri recognizes as well as the language that she uses to speak. To change the Siri language:

1. Touch the  icon. The Settings screen appears.
2. Touch **General**. The General Settings screen appears.
3. Touch **Siri**. The Siri Settings screen appears, as shown in **Figure 9**.
4. Touch **Language**. A list of available Siri languages appears, as shown in **Figure 10**.

5. Touch a language. The selected language will be used for Siri.

Note: Press and hold the **Home** *button to activate Siri. The Siri screen appears, as shown in* **Figure 11**.

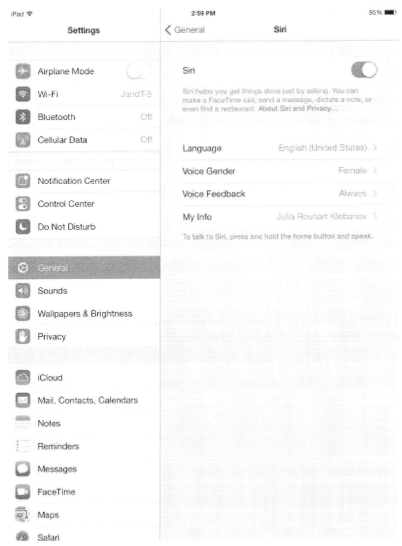

Figure 9: Siri Settings Screen

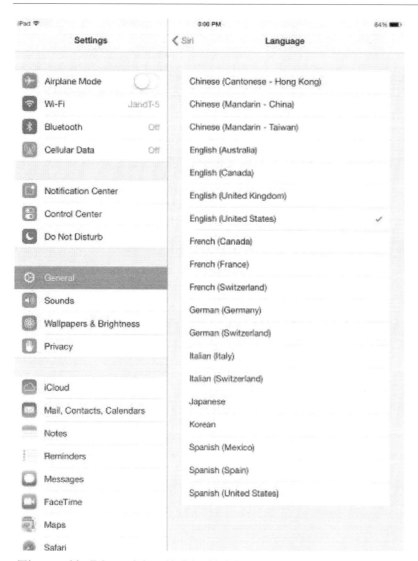

Figure 10: List of Available Siri Languages

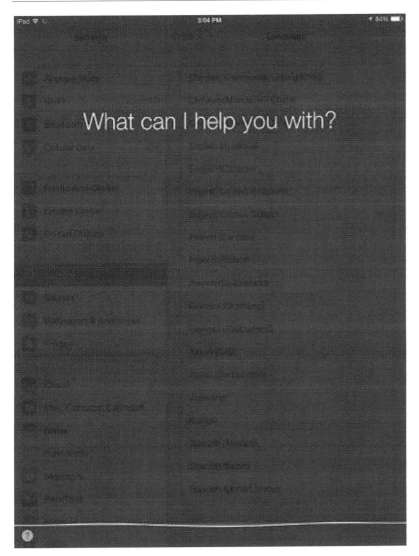

Figure 11: Siri Screen

6. Changing the Keyboard Layout

The layout of the keyboard in most languages can be changed according to personal preference. For instance, the English keyboard can be set display in default QWERTY, as shown in **Figure 12**, AZERTY, as shown in **Figure 13**, or QWERTZ as shown in **Figure 14**. To change the Keyboard Layout:

1. Touch the 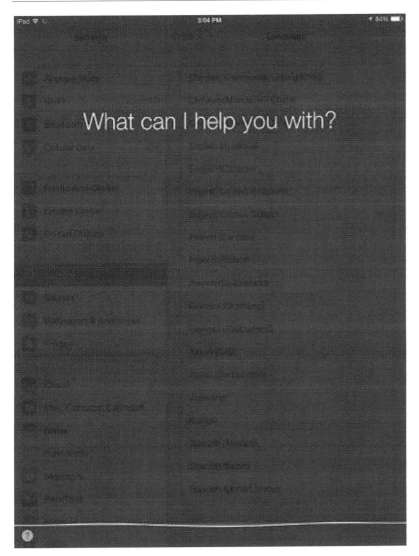 icon. The Settings screen appears.
2. Touch **General**. The General Settings screen appears.
3. Scroll down and touch **Keyboard**. The Keyboard Settings screen appears.

4. Touch **Keyboards**. The Keyboards screen appears.
5. Touch the language of the keyboard that you wish to change. The Keyboard Layout screen appears.
6. Touch the desired layout. The new Keyboard Layout is set.

Figure 12: QWERTY Keyboard

Figure 13: AZERTY Keyboard

Figure 14: QWERTZ Keyboard

7. Turning the Split Keyboard On or Off

The Split Keyboard is a feature that allows you to type on a more ergonomic keyboard. Refer to *"Using the Split Keyboard"* on page 250 to learn how to use it. By default, the Split Keyboard is turned on. To turn the Split Keyboard on or off:

1. Touch the ⚙ icon. The Settings screen appears.
2. Touch **General**. The General Settings screen appears.
3. Scroll down and touch **Keyboard**. The Keyboard Settings screen appears.

4. Touch the ⬤ switch next to 'Split Keyboard'. The ⬤ switch appears, and the Split Keyboard is turned off.

5. Touch the ⬤ switch next to 'Split Keyboard'. The ⬤ switch appears, and the Split Keyboard is turned on.

Adjusting General Settings

Table of Contents

1. Changing Auto-Lock Settings

The iPad can lock itself when it is idle in order to save battery life and to avoid unintentionally pressing buttons. When it is locked, the iPad can still receive calls and text messages. By default, the iPad is set to automatically lock after one minute. To change the length of time that will pass before the iPad locks itself:

1. Touch the ![icon] icon. The Settings screen appears, as shown in **Figure 1**.
2. Touch **General**. The General Settings screen appears, as shown in **Figure 2**.
3. Touch **Auto-Lock**. The Auto-Lock Settings screen appears, as shown in **Figure 3**.
4. Touch an amount of time, or touch **Never** if you do not want the iPad to automatically lock itself. The change is applied and the iPad will wait the selected amount of time before automatically locking itself.

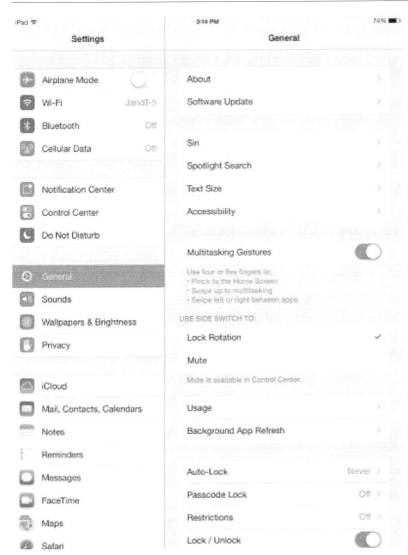

Figure 1: Settings Screen

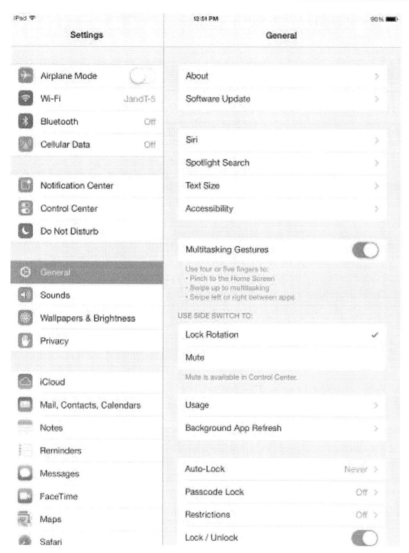

Figure 2: General Settings Screen

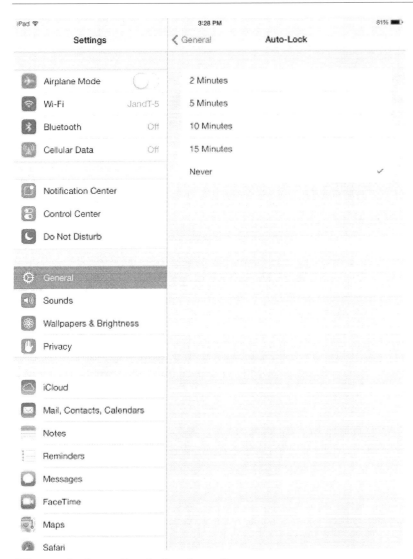

Figure 3: Auto-Lock Settings Screen

2. Adjusting the Brightness

You may wish to increase the brightness of the screen on your iPad when you are in a sunny area. On the other hand, you may wish to decrease the brightness in a dark area to conserve battery life and to keep yourself from being blinded. You can also turn Auto-Brightness on or off, which will determine whether or not the iPad automatically sets the brightness based on the lighting conditions. To adjust the brightness:

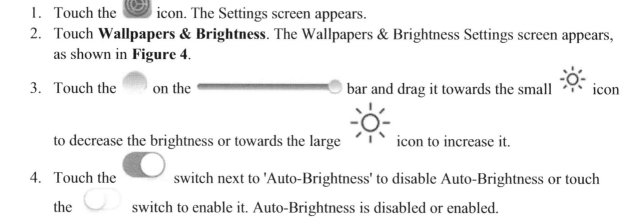

1. Touch the 　　 icon. The Settings screen appears.
2. Touch **Wallpapers & Brightness**. The Wallpapers & Brightness Settings screen appears, as shown in **Figure 4**.
3. Touch the 　　 on the ━━━━━━━━━ bar and drag it towards the small ☼ icon

    to decrease the brightness or towards the large ☼ icon to increase it.
4. Touch the 　　 switch next to 'Auto-Brightness' to disable Auto-Brightness or touch

    the 　　 switch to enable it. Auto-Brightness is disabled or enabled.

Note: While Auto-Brightness is enabled, you can still temporarily adjust the brightness of the screen. However, as soon as the lighting conditions change, the iPad will automatically change the brightness.

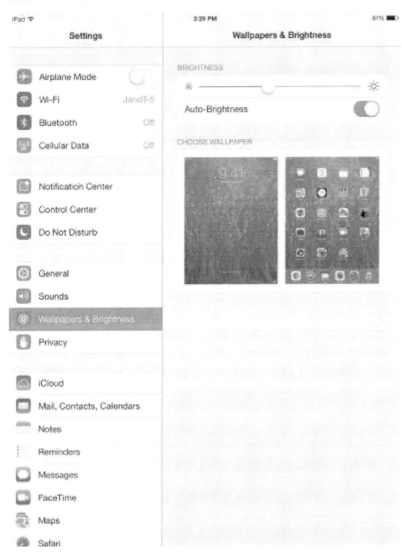

Figure 4: Wallpapers & Brightness Settings Screen

3. Assigning a Passcode Lock

You may choose to lock the iPad using a password in order to protect any sensitive information. The iPad can prompt for a four-digit or alphanumeric password.

To set up a passcode lock:

1. Touch the ⚙ icon. The Settings screen appears.
2. Touch **General**. The General Settings screen appears.
3. Touch **Passcode Lock**. The Passcode Lock screen appears, as shown in **Figure 5**.
4. Touch **Turn Passcode On**. The Set Passcode screen appears, as shown in **Figure 6**, if the Simple Passcode feature is turned on. The Set Password screen appears, as shown in **Figure 7**, if the Simple Passcode feature is turned off.
5. Enter a passcode. A confirmation screen appears.
6. Enter the passcode again. The new passcode is set.
7. Touch one of the following options on the Passcode Lock screen to change the corresponding setting:

   - **Require Passcode** - Set the time the iPad waits before asking the user for the passcode. It is recommended to choose the default, **Immediately**, since an unauthorized user will not have access to your iPad for any period of time if this option is chosen. Choosing one of the other options causes the iPad to wait a set amount of time after being locked before requiring a passcode.
   - **Simple Passcode** - Allows you to enter a four-digit passcode. When turned off, you must enter an alphanumeric password when setting the passcode
   - **Erase Data** - Erases all data after a user enters the passcode incorrectly ten times in a row.

Warning: You will not be able to recover your data if the 'Erase Data' feature is on and an incorrect passcode is entered ten times consecutively.

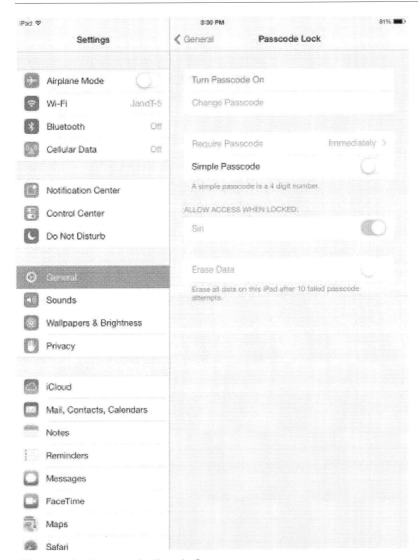

Figure 5: Passcode Lock Screen

Figure 6: Set Passcode Screen

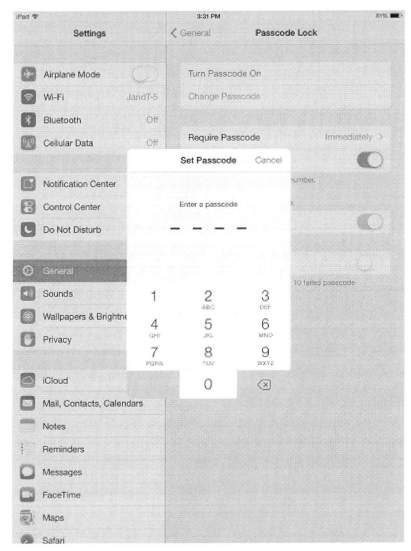

Figure 7: Set Password Screen

4 Turning 24-Hour Mode On or Off

The iPad can display the time in regular 12-hour mode or in 24-hour mode, commonly referred to as military time. To turn 24-hour mode on or off:

1. Touch the icon. The Settings screen appears.
2. Touch **General**. The General Settings screen appears.
3. Scroll down and touch **Date & Time**. The Date & Time screen appears, as shown in **Figure 8**.

4. Touch the ⬤ switch next to '24-Hour Time'. The ⬤ switch appears 24-Hour mode is turned on.

5. Touch the ⬤ switch next to '24-Hour Time'. The ⬤ switch appears and 24-Hour mode is turned off.

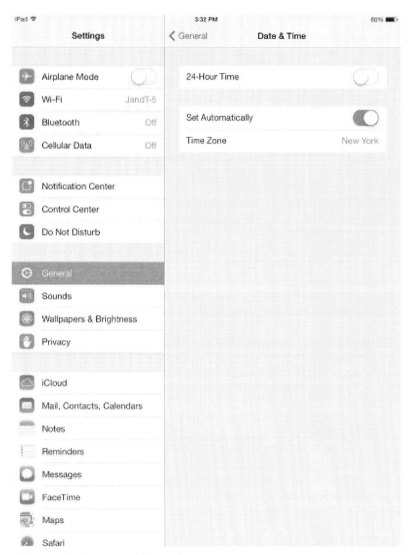

Figure 8: Date & Time Screen

5. Resetting the Home Screen Layout

You can reset the Home screen on your iPad to look like it did when you first purchased it. To reset the Home Screen Layout:

Note: Resetting the Home screen layout does not delete any applications, but simply rearranges them.

1. Touch the icon. The Settings screen appears.
2. Touch **General**. The General Settings screen appears.
3. Scroll down and touch **Reset**. The Reset screen appears, as shown in **Figure 9**.
4. Touch **Reset Home Screen Layout**. A confirmation dialog appears.
5. Touch **Reset**. The Home Screen Layout is reset. Alternatively, touch **Cancel** if you have changed your mind.

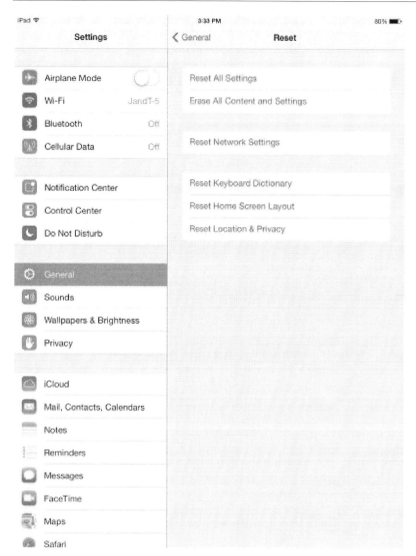

Figure 9: Reset Screen

---

6. Resetting All Settings

You can reset all of the settings on your iPad to the state they were in when you first purchased it. To reset all settings:

Note: Resetting the settings will NOT delete any data or applications from your iPad.

1. Touch the ⚙ icon. The Settings screen appears.
2. Touch **General**. The General Settings screen appears.

3. Scroll down and touch **Reset**. The Reset screen appears.
4. Touch **Reset All Settings**. A confirmation dialog appears. You will also need to enter your passcode, if you have one.
5. Touch **Reset**. All settings are reset to defaults.

7. Erasing and Restoring the iPad

You can delete all of the data and reset all settings to completely restore the iPad to its original condition. To erase and restore the iPad to its original condition:

Warning: Any erased data is not recoverable. Make sure to back up all of the data that you wish to keep.

1. Touch the ⊚ icon. The Settings screen appears.
2. Touch **General**. The General Settings screen appears.
3. Touch **Reset**. The Reset screen appears.
4. Touch **Erase All Content and Settings**. A confirmation dialog appears.
5. Touch **Erase**. Data on the iPad is erased, and the iPad is restored to its original condition.

8. Changing the Function of the Side Switch

The Side switch on the iPad can be used to perform one of two possible functions. The Side switch can lock and unlock the screen rotation, which prevents or allows screen rotation when the iPad is rotated. Alternatively, it can turn the Mute function on or off, which mutes all sounds. To change the functionality of the Side switch:

1. Touch the ⊚ icon. The Settings screen appears.
2. Touch **General**. The General Settings screen appears.

3. Touch **Lock Rotation** under 'USE SIDE SWITCH TO:'. The Side switch will be used to lock and unlock screen rotation. When the 🔒 icon appears, screen rotation is locked. When the 🔓 icon appears, screen rotation is unlocked.

4. Touch **Mute**. The Side switch will be used to turn Mute on or off. When the ⌇ icon

appears, Mute is turned on. When the ⌇ icon appears, Mute is turned off.

9. Turning Multitasking Gestures On or Off

The iPad allows you to use multi-touch gestures to navigate the screens, using four or five fingers. Refer to *"Using Multitasking Gestures"* on page 251 to learn how to use gestures. By default, Multitasking Gestures are turned on. To turn Multitasking Gestures on or off:

1. Touch the ⚙ icon. The Settings screen appears.
2. Touch **General**. The General Settings screen appears.

3. Touch the ⬤ switch next to 'Multitasking Gestures'. The ⬭ switch appears and Multitasking Gestures are turned off.

4. Touch the ⬭ switch next to 'Multitasking Gestures'. The ⬤ switch appears and Multitasking Gestures are turned on.

10. Turning the iPad Cover Lock On or Off

The iPad can automatically lock and unlock itself when you close or open your Smart Cover. By default, the iPad Cover Lock is turned on. To turn the iPad Cover Lock on or off:

1. Touch the ⚙ icon. The Settings screen appears.
2. Touch **General**. The General Settings screen appears.

3. Touch the ⬤ switch next to 'iPad Cover Lock / Unlock'. The ⬭ switch appears and the iPad Cover Lock is turned off.

4. Touch the ⬭ switch next to 'iPad Cover Lock / Unlock'. The ⬤ switch appears and the iPad Cover Lock is turned on.

Adjusting Accessibility Settings

Table of Contents

1. Managing Vision Accessibility Features

Vision accessibility features allow people with visual disabilities to use the iPad with greater ease. To manage vision accessibility features:

1. Touch the icon. The Settings screen appears, as shown in **Figure 1**.
2. Touch **General**. The General Settings screen appears, as shown in **Figure 2**.
3. Touch **Accessibility**. The Accessibility Settings screen appears, as shown in **Figure 3**.
4. Touch one of the following options to turn vision accessibility features on or off:
   - **VoiceOver** - This feature speaks an item on the screen when you touch it once, activates it when you touch it twice, and scrolls through a list or page of text when you touch the screen with three fingers.
   - **Zoom** - This feature zooms in on an item when you touch the screen twice using three fingers, moves around when you drag three fingers on the screen, and changes the level of zoom when you touch the screen with three fingers twice and drag.
   - **Invert Colors** - This feature inverts all of the colors on the screen. For instance, black text on a white screen becomes white text on a black screen.
   - **Speak Selection** - This feature allows all text on the screen to be spoken aloud when you select it and touch **Speak**.
   - **Speak Auto-text** - This feature speaks every auto-correction or auto-capitalization as you enter text in any text field, including text messages and emails.
   - **Larger Type** - This feature increases the default size of the font. Use the font slider to adjust the default font size.
   - **Bold Text** - This feature makes all text on the iPad bold in order to make it easier to read. Enabling or disabling this feature requires you to restart the iPad.
   - **Increase Contrast** - This feature improves the contrast on certain backgrounds in order to make it easier to read certain text.

- **Reduce Motion** - This feature controls menu and icon animation effects, and is especially useful for people with epilepsy.

- **On/Off Labels** - This feature turns and switches into and switches, respectively.

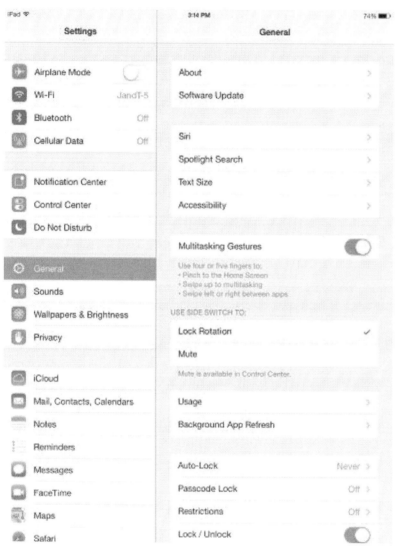

Figure 1: Settings Screen

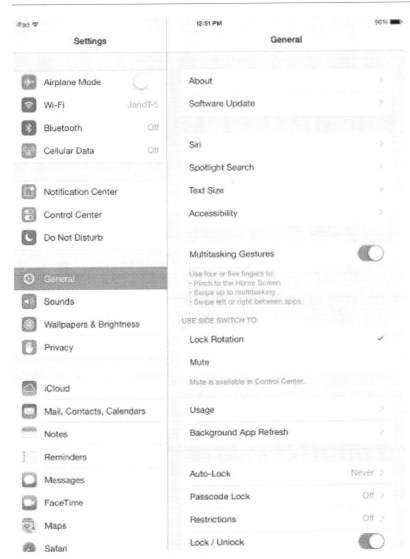

Figure 2: General Settings Screen

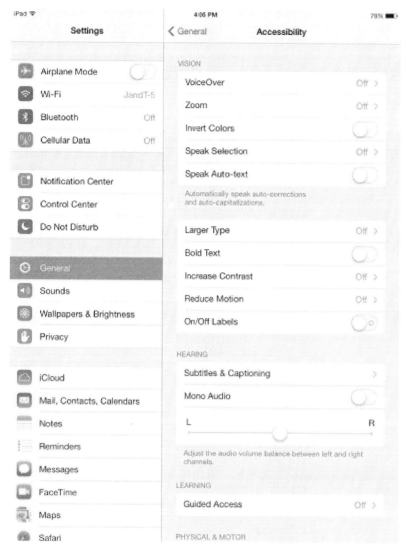

Figure 3: Accessibility Settings Screen

---

2. Managing Hearing Accessibility Features

Hearing accessibility features allow people with hearing disabilities to use the iPad with greater ease. To manage hearing accessibility features:

- Touch the 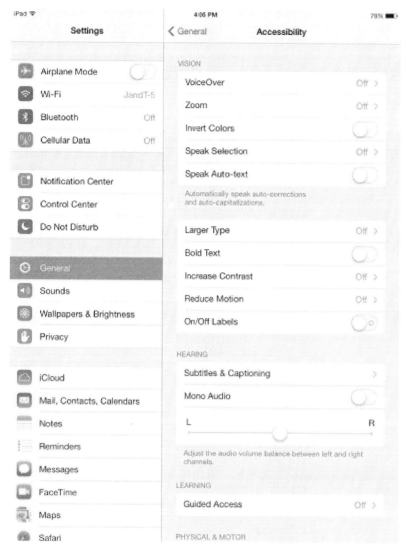 icon. The Settings screen appears.
- Touch **General**. The General Settings screen appears.

- Touch **Accessibility**. The Accessibility Settings screen appears

- Touch one of the following options to turn hearing accessibility features on or off:

  - **Subtitles & Captioning** - This feature allows subtitles and closed captioning to be enabled for videos, where available.
  - **Mono Audio** - This feature turns off stereo audio, leaving only one speaker working.

3. Turning Guided Access On or Off

Guided Access is a feature that is made for people with learning disabilities, allowing the user to stay in a single application and control the features that are available. To turn Guided Access on or off:

1. Touch the [icon] icon. The Settings screen appears.
2. Touch **General**. The General Settings screen appears.
3. Touch **Accessibility**. The Accessibility Settings screen appears.
4. Scroll down and touch **Guided Access**. The Guided Access Settings screen appears, as shown in **Figure 4**.
5. Touch the [switch] switch next to 'Guided Access'. Guided Access is turned on.
6. Touch **Set Passcode** to set up a passcode that will allow you to exit the application when you are done using it.

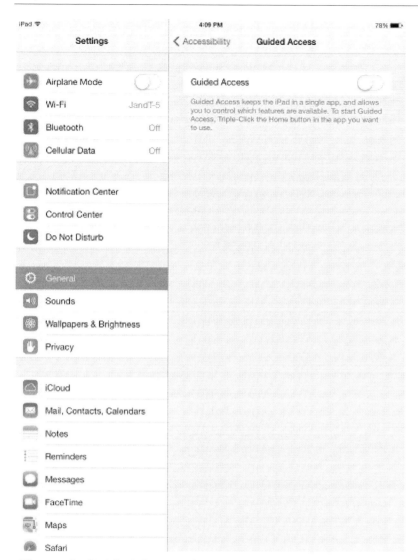

Figure 4: Guided Access Settings Screen

4. Managing Physical & Motor Accessibility Features

Physical and Motor accessibility features allow people with motor disabilities to use the iPad with greater ease. To manage physical & motor accessibility features:

- Touch the ⚙ icon. The Settings screen appears.
- Touch **General**. The General Settings screen appears.
- Touch **Accessibility**. The Accessibility Settings screen appears.
- Touch one of the following options to turn physical and motor accessibility features on or off:

  - **Switch Control** - This feature allows an adaptive accessory to be used to highlight items on the screen to control the functions of the iPad. The Switch Control screen allows various settings, such as timing, switch stabilization, point scanning, audio, and visual settings, to be adjusted.
  - **Assistive Touch** - This feature allows you to create custom gestures in order to access various services on the iPad.
  - **Home-click Speed** - This feature allows you to slow down the speed at which you need to press the Home button to access certain features.

Adjusting Photo and Video Settings

Table of Contents

1. Turning Photo Stream On or Off

Photo Stream allows you to instantly load photos that you have taken on your iPad to your other registered Apple devices. It accomplishes this by automatically uploading them to the iCloud and then downloading them to other devices registered to the same Apple ID. To turn Photo Stream on or off:

1. Touch the 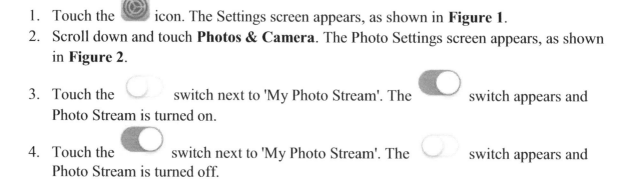 icon. The Settings screen appears, as shown in **Figure 1**.
2. Scroll down and touch **Photos & Camera**. The Photo Settings screen appears, as shown in **Figure 2**.

3. Touch the ⬭ switch next to 'My Photo Stream'. The ⬭ switch appears and Photo Stream is turned on.

4. Touch the ⬭ switch next to 'My Photo Stream'. The ⬭ switch appears and Photo Stream is turned off.

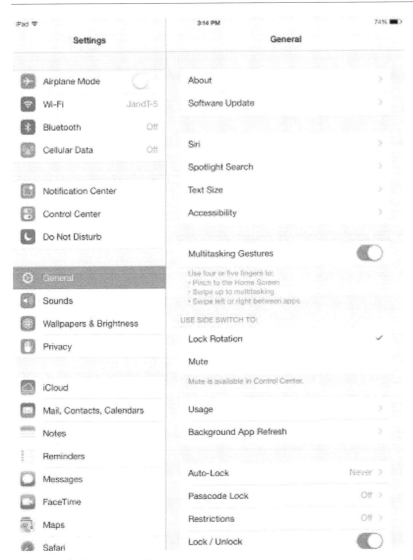

Figure 1: Settings Screen

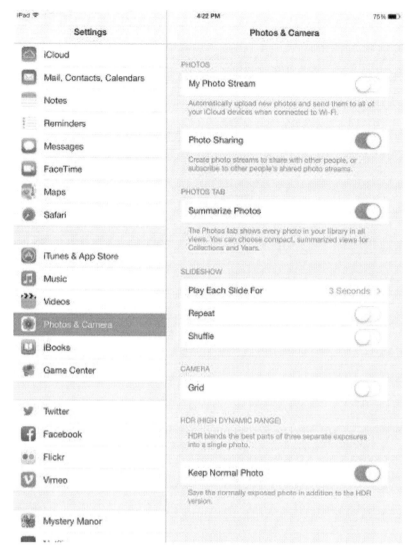

Figure 2: Photo Settings Screen

2. Customizing Slideshow Settings

You can customize the slideshow settings on your iPad. Refer to *"Viewing a Slideshow"* on page 43 to learn how to turn on a slideshow. To customize Slideshow settings:

1. Touch the 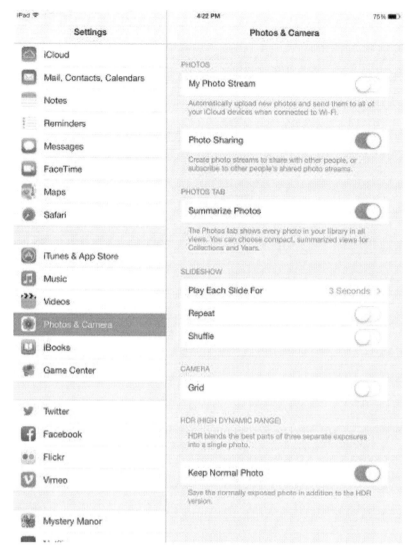 icon. The Settings screen appears.
2. Scroll down and touch **Photos & Camera**. The Photo Settings screen appears.
3. Touch one of the following options or the On/Off switch next to one of the options under the 'Slideshow' section to change the corresponding setting:

- **Play Each Slide For** - Sets the amount of time that each photo remains on the screen during a slideshow.
- **Repeat** - Sets the slideshow to start again from the beginning of the current album after reaching the end.
- **Shuffle** - Sets the photos to appear in random order during a slideshow.

Note: Turning on both 'Repeat' and 'Shuffle' at the same time plays your photos continuously and in random order.

3. Customizing High Dynamic Range (HDR) Camera Settings

When taking photos with the iPad, you can enable HDR, which will improve picture quality by taking several photos and averaging the amount of light. This process produces a photo with much more realistic lighting than one taken by a non-HDR camera. To turn on HDR, touch **HDR Off** on the right side of the screen while the camera is running. When HDR is turned on, a non-HDR copy of each photo is stored by default. To customize HDR settings:

1. Touch the ⚙ icon. The Settings screen appears.
2. Scroll down and touch **Photos and Camera**. The Photo Settings screen appears.
3. Touch the ⬤ switch next to 'Keep Normal Photo'. The ◯ switch appears and the iPad will now delete non-HDR photos while keeping the HDR copy.
4. Touch the ◯ switch next to 'Keep Normal Photo'. The ⬤ switch appears and the iPad will keep the non-HDR photo in addition to the HDR copy when taking photos.

Note: An HDR photo takes up more memory on your device than a non-HDR one.

4. Customizing Video Playback Settings

After a video is stopped (not paused), the iPad can resume playing it from the beginning or from where you last left off. To customize Video Playback settings:

1. Touch the ⚙ icon. The Settings screen appears.
2. Scroll down and touch **Videos**. The Video Settings screen appears, as shown in **Figure 3**.
3. Touch **Start Playing**. The Start Playing screen appears, as shown in **Figure 4**.
4. Touch **From Beginning**. Videos will now resume from the beginning.
5. Touch **Where Left Off**. Videos will now resume where they last left off.

6. Touch **Videos** in the upper left-hand corner of the screen. Your video playback selection is saved.

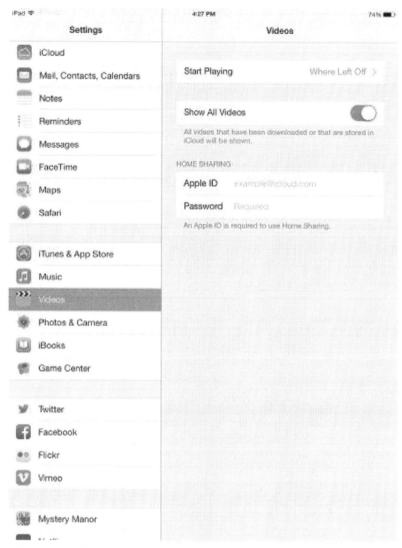

Figure 3: Video Settings Screen

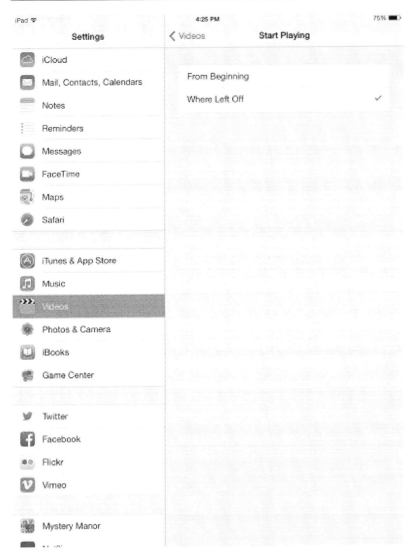

Figure 4: Start Playing Screen

5. Choosing which Videos Appear in the Videos Application

The Videos application can either display all of your videos, both in the Cloud and on your device, or just the videos on your device. To choose which videos appear in the Videos application:

1. Touch the ⊚ icon. The Settings screen appears.
2. Scroll down and touch **Videos**. The Video Settings screen appears.

3. Touch the ⬭ switch next to 'Show All Videos'. The ⬤ switch appears and all videos, both on your device and in the Cloud will appear in the Videos application.

4. Touch the ⬤ switch next to 'Show All Videos'. The ⬭ switch appears and only videos on your device will appear in the Videos application.

Tips and Tricks

Table of Contents

1. Maximizing Battery Life

There are several things you can do to increase the battery life of the iPad:

- Lock the iPad whenever you are not using it. To lock the iPad, press the **Sleep/Wake** button at the top of the phone. Refer to *"Button Layout"* on page 8 for the location of the Sleep/Wake button.
- Keep the Auto-lock feature on and set it to a small amount of time to wait before locking the phone when it is idle. Refer to *"Changing Auto-Lock Settings"* on page 216 to learn how to change Auto-lock settings.

- Turn down the brightness and turn off Auto-Brightness. Refer to *"Adjusting the Brightness"* on page 220 to learn how.
- Turn on Airplane mode in areas where there is little or no signal, as the iPad will continually try to search for service. Refer to *"Turning Airplane Mode On or Off"* on page 184 to learn how to turn on Airplane Mode.
- Make sure to let the battery drain completely and then charge it fully at least once a month. This will help both short-term and long-term battery life.
- Turn off 4G when it is not in use. Refer to *"Turning 4G On or Off"* on page 188 to learn how.
- Turn off Wi-Fi when it is not in use. Refer to *"Setting Up Wi-Fi"* on page 12 to learn how.
- Turn off Location Services when they are not in use. Refer to *"Turning Location Services On or Off"* on page 185 to learn how.

2. Taking a Screenshot

To capture what is on the screen and save it as a photo, press and hold the **Home** button and the **Sleep/Wake** button at the same time. Release the buttons and the screen will momentarily flash a white color. The screenshot is saved to the 'Camera Roll' album.

3. Scrolling to the Top of a Screen

Touch anywhere in the notification bar at the very top of the screen to quickly scroll to the top of a list, website, etc. The notification bar is where the time and battery meter are located.

4. Saving an Image While Browsing the Internet

To save an image from Safari to the iPad, touch and hold the picture until the Image menu appears. Touch **Save Image**. The image is saved to the Camera Roll album.

5. Inserting a Period

When typing a sentence, touch the space bar twice quickly to insert a period and a space at the end of it.

6. Navigating the Home Screens

Typically, you get to another Home screen by touching the screen and sliding your finger to the left or right. Alternatively, touch one of the gray dots at the bottom of a Home screen to go to the next one.

7. Typing Alternate Characters

When typing a sentence, insert other characters, such as Á or Ñ, by touching and holding the base letter. A menu of characters appears above the letter. Touch a character to insert it.

8. Deleting Recently Typed Text

This feature is quite a secret. If you have just typed several lines of text and do not want any of it, just give the iPad a good shake. A menu appears asking whether to undo the typing. Touch **Undo**. The typed text is erased. Give the iPad another shake to redo the typing. This works in any application or while text messaging.

9. Resetting the iPad

If the iPad or an application freezes up or is acting strangely, you may wish to reset the iPad. This will NOT wipe any data, but will simply restart the operating system. To reset the iPad, hold the **Home** button and **Sleep/Wake** button together until the iPad completely shuts off. Continue to hold the buttons until the logo appears. The iPad resets and starts up.

10. Taking Notes

A convenient way to take notes is by using the built-in Notes application and emailing the notes to yourself. To take notes, touch the ▭ icon. Touch the ◪ button at the top right of the screen to add a note. Touch the ⬆ icon at the bottom of the screen and then touch **Email** to email the note.

11. Recovering Signal After Being in an Area with No Service

Sometimes the iPad has trouble finding signal after returning from an area where AT&T or Verizon was not available. This issue can sometimes be fixed by turning Airplane Mode on and then back off. Refer to *"Turning Airplane Mode On or Off"* on page 184 to learn how.

12. Deleting a Song in the Music Application

To delete a song from your iPad, touch the song and swipe your finger to the left. 'DELETE' appears. Touch **DELETE**. The song is deleted.

13. Taking a Picture from the Lock Screen

To take a picture without unlocking the phone, touch the 📷 icon in the lower right-hand corner of the screen and slide your finger up. The camera turns on. Press the **Volume Up** button. The camera takes a picture.

14. Assigning a Custom Ringtone to a Contact

You can assign a custom ringtone to any contact in the Phonebook. To assign a ringtone to a contact:

1. Touch the 👤 icon. The Phonebook appears.

2. Find and touch the contact to whom you wish to assign a custom ringtone. The Contact Info screen appears. Refer to *"Finding a Contact"* on page 124 to learn how.

3. Touch **Edit** in the upper right-hand corner of the screen. The Contact Editing screen appears.

4. Touch **Ringtone**. A list of available ringtones appears.

5. Touch a ringtone. The ringtone plays.

6. Touch **Done** in the upper right-hand corner of the screen. The ringtone is selected and the Contact Editing screen appears.

7. Touch **Done** in the upper right-hand corner of the screen. The ringtone is assigned to the contact.

Note: Refer to "Buying Tones in iTunes" *on page 84 to learn how to purchase additional ringtones.*

15. Opening the Photos Application without Closing the Camera

To open the Photos application while the camera is turned on, touch the photo thumbnail in the bottom right-hand corner of the screen.

16. Inserting Emoticons

The Emoji keyboard contains over 460 new emoticons that can be used when entering text. To learn how to add the Emoji keyboard, refer to *"Adding an International Keyboard"* on page

205 and touch **Emoji** in step 6. After adding the Emoji keyboard, touch the ⊕ key at the bottom of the virtual keyboard to switch to the Emoji keyboard while typing. The Emoji keyboard appears.

17. Hiding the Keyboard in an Application

While using the keyboard, you can hide it to view more of the screen at once. Touch anywhere just above the keyboard, and slide your finger down to it. The keyboard is hidden.

18. Controlling Web Surfing Using Gestures

Instead of touching the ⟨ and ⟩ buttons to go back and forward, respectively, you can touch the screen and slide your finger the left or right, respectively.

19. Pausing an Application Download

If you are downloading more than one application at a time, you may wish to pause one of the downloads so that one of the other applications downloads first. To pause an application download, touch the application icon of the application that you wish to pause. Touch the icon again to resume the download.

20. Making a Quick Note for a Contact

You may take a quick note for a contact without having to edit the entire contents of the contact's information. To make a quick note for a contact, touch **Notes** under 'Facetime' on the contact's information screen. Touch **All Contacts** in the upper left-hand corner of the screen to save the note.

21. Using the Split Keyboard

The Split Keyboard is a feature that allows you to type more comfortably on a more ergonomic keyboard, which is split into two halves on the left and right sides of the screen. To use the Split

Keyboard, touch and hold the [⌨] key in the lower right-hand corner of the screen and slide

your finger up on the screen. The keyboard is split. Touch and hold the [⌨] key and slide your finger down on the screen to return to using the default keyboard. If you cannot split the keyboard, make sure that the feature is turned on. Refer to *"Turning the Split Keyboard On or Off"* on page 215 to learn how to turn on the Split Keyboard.

22. Using Multitasking Gestures

The iPad allows you to switch between applications and return to the Home screen by gesturing with four or five fingers. The following multitasking gestures can be used:

- Touch the screen with four fingers and slide them to the left or right to switch to another open application.
- Touch the screen with four fingers and slide them up to view a list of open applications.
- Touch the screen with five fingers spread apart and move them together to go to the Home screen.

Troubleshooting

Table of Contents

1. iPad does not turn on

If the iPad does not power on, try one or more of the following tips:

- **Recharge the iPad** - Use the included wall charger to charge the battery. If the battery power is extremely low, the screen will not turn on for several minutes. Do NOT use the USB port on your computer to charge the iPad.
- **Reset the iPad** - This method will not erase any data. Hold down the **Home** button and **Sleep/Wake** button at the same time for 10 seconds. Keep holding the two buttons

  until the logo appears and the iPad restarts.

2. iPad is not responding

If the iPad is frozen or is not responding, try one or more of the following. These steps solve most problems on the iPad.

- **Turn the iPad Off and then Back On** - If the iPad is still frozen, try pressing the **Sleep/Wake** button to turn the iPad off. Keep holding the **Sleep/Wake** Button until "Slide to Power Off" appears. Slide your finger from left to right over the text. The iPad turns off. After the screen is completely black, press the **Sleep/Wake** button again to turn the iPad back on.
- **Restart the iPad** - Hold the **Home** button and **Sleep/Wake** button at the same time for 10 seconds or until the [logo] logo appears.
- **Remove Media** - Some downloaded applications or music may freeze up the iPad. Try deleting some of the media that may be problematic after restarting the iPad. Refer to *"Deleting an Application"* on page 146 to learn how to delete an application. You may also erase all data at once by doing the following:

Warning: Once erased, data cannot be recovered (except for applications). Make sure you back up any files that you wish to keep.

1. Touch the [icon] icon. The Settings screen appears.
2. Touch **General**. The General Settings screen appears.
3. Touch **Reset**. The Reset screen appears.
4. Touch **Erase All Content and Settings**. A confirmation dialog appears.

3. Can't make a FaceTime call

If the iPad cannot make outgoing FaceTime calls, try one of the following:

- If "No Service" is shown at the top left of the screen, the network does not cover you in your location. Try moving to a different location, or even to a different part of the building.
- Turn off Airplane Mode if you have it turned on. If that does not work, try turning Airplane Mode on for 15 seconds and then turning it off. Refer to *"Turning Airplane Mode On or Off"* on page 184 to learn how.
- Make sure that Wi-Fi or 4G (4G models only) is turned on. Refer to *"Setting Up Wi-Fi"* on page 12 or *"Turning 4G On or Off"* on page 188 to learn how.
- Turn the iPad off and back on.

4. Can't surf the web

If you have no internet access, there may be little or no service in your area. Try moving to a different location or turning on 4G or Wi-Fi. Refer to *"Turning 4G On or Off"* on page 188 to learn how to turn on 4G or to *"Setting Up Wi-Fi"* on page 12 to learn how to turn on Wi-Fi. If you still can't get online, refer to *"iPad is not responding"* on page 252 for further assistance.

5. Screen or keyboard does not rotate

If the screen does not rotate or the full, horizontal keyboard does not appear when you rotate the iPad, it may be one of these issues:

- The application does not support the horizontal view.
- The iPad is lying flat. Hold the iPad upright to change the view in applications that support it.
- The rotation lock is on. Press the **Home** button twice quickly and scroll all the way to the left to check. The rotation is locked if the icon looks like this: 🔘. Touch the 🔘 icon. Screen rotation is unlocked.

6. iTunes does not detect iPad when connected to a computer

If iTunes does not detect the iPad when connecting it to your computer, try using a different USB port. If that does not work, turn the iPad off and on again while it is plugged in to the computer. If the iPad indicates that it is connected, the problem might be with your computer. Try restarting your computer or reinstalling iTunes. Otherwise, refer to *"iPad is not responding"* on page 252 for assistance.

7. iPad does not ring or play music

Make sure that the volume is turned up. Refer to *"Button Layout"* on page 8 to find the Volume Controls. Check whether you can still hear sound through headphones. The headphone jack is located on the top of the iPad. If you can hear sound through headphones, try inserting the headphones and taking them out several times. Sometimes the sensor in the headphone jack malfunctions.

8. Camera does not work

If the iPad camera is not functioning correctly, try one of the following:

- Clean the camera lens with a polishing cloth.
- Take off any cases or accessories that may interfere with the camera lens on the back of the iPad.
- Hold the iPad steady when taking a picture. A shaky hand often results in a blurry picture. Try leaning against a stationary object to stabilize your hand.

- If you cannot find the icon on your Home screen, try the following:

  1. Touch the icon. The Settings screen appears.
  2. Touch **General**. The General Settings screen appears.
  3. Touch **Restrictions**. The Restrictions screen appears.
  4. Touch **Disable Restrictions**. All restrictions are disabled and the camera should now work.

9. iPad shows the White Screen of Death

If the iPad screen has gone completely white, try restarting or restoring the iPad. Refer to *"iPad is not responding"* on page 252 to learn how.

10. "iPad needs to cool down" message appears

If you leave the iPad in your car on a hot day or expose it to direct sunlight for too long, one of the following may happen:

- Device stops charging
- Weak signal
- Screen dims
- "iPad needs to cool down" message appears
- iPad breaks completely

Before using the iPad, allow it to cool. The iPad works best in temperatures between 32°F and 95°F (0°C to 35°C). While it is turned off, store the iPad at temperatures between -4°F and 113°F (-20°C to 45°C).

11. Display does not adjust brightness automatically

If the iPad does not brighten in bright conditions or does not become dimmer in dark conditions, try taking any cases or accessories off. A case may block the light sensor, located at the top of the iPad near the camera. Also, check to make sure that Auto-Brightness is turned on. Refer to *"Adjusting the Brightness"* on page 220 to learn how to turn on Auto-Brightness.

Index

E

L

M

F

G

H

N

I

U

V

W

Other Books from the Author of the Help Me Series, Charles Hughes

Help Me! Guide to the iPhone 5S

Help Me! Guide to the Nexus 7

Help Me! Guide to the Galaxy S4

Help Me! Guide to the Kindle Fire HDX

Help Me! Guide to the HTC One

Help Me! Guide to the iPhone 4

Help Me! Guide to the iPod Touch

Help Me! Guide to the iPad Mini

Help Me! Guide to the Kindle Touch

Help Me! Guide to the Samsumg Galaxy Note

Help Me! Guide to the iPad Air